TASMANIA'S UNIQUE TOURIST ACCOMMODATION
Australia's Best Kept Secret

Tasmania's Unique Tourist Accommodation

AUSTRALIA'S BEST KEPT SECRET

Michael Hamman & Ann-Marie Alibrandi

HILL OF CONTENT

MELBOURNE

First published in Australia 1989
by Hill of Content Publishing
86 Bourke Street, Melbourne 3000

© Copyright Michael Hamman & Ann-Marie Alibrandi 1989

Illustrated by: Candace Wright

Cover design by: Jane Wallace-Mitchell
Cover photograph: Taranna House, Taranna

Printed in Australia by Australian Print Group

Cataloguing-in-publication data
Hamman, Michael, 1957-   .
   Tasmania's unique tourist accommodation.

   Includes index.
   ISBN 0 85572 186 3.

   1. Hotels, taverns, etc.—Tasmania—Directories. 2.
   Tasmania—Description and travel—1976-   -
   Guide-books. I. Alibrandi, Ann-Marie, 1962-   . II.
   Title.

647′.9494601

TABLE OF CONTENTS

TO OUR PARENTS

ACKNOWLEDGEMENTS

We would like to thank all of our newly-found friends in Tasmania who were so hospitable and provided us with all the information necessary to compile this book. Also, a big thank you to those who kept us full with plenty of tea and homemade biscuits. Special thanks to Cathie and Steve in Melbourne for their culinary support and 'Aussie' language interpretations.

INTRODUCTION

Some people just can't keep a secret . . .

Spend a quiet evening in an overstuffed chair before a crackling open fire while glancing through a century old newspaper by dim candlelight. The stillness is almost piercing and the silence is broken only by the symphony of frogs and crickets outside your tiny sandstone cottage . . .

Enjoy a crisp country morning from the warmth of an 1890s farmhouse; delight in watching your children learn the workings of a farm, perhaps even marvel in the wonder of a tiny lamb being born . . .

Awaken in the morning to the laughter of a kookaburra perched in the apple tree outside your window. Smell hand-cured bacon sizzling in the kitchen. Later, take a picnic lunch and a bottle of delicious Tasmanian wine into the neighboring countryside and enjoy the solitude while rekindling an old romance or starting a new one . . .

After a day of sightseeing in the historic Midlands area, return to your suite in a majestic Victorian manor and enjoy the postcard view from your bay window. In the morning, enjoy the company of other travellers over a hearty breakfast featuring farm-fresh eggs and homemade jams. Fresh flowers accent the crisp linen tablecloth and fine china . . .

These are the secrets of Tasmania.

You can spend your holiday in an ordinary motel room where you are known by your credit card number rather than your name, or you can just as casily (and often less expensively) enjoy the unique pleasures of dozens of retreats like these.

Tasmania offers a broad range of truly unique accommodation. You can enjoy the intimacy of your own 1830s cottage, stay in what was once the stables of a colonial bakery, or relax in a stone schoolhouse built by convicts in the 1850s. You can even retrace the steps of some of those unfortunate convicts when you stay at an old outstation of the infamous Port Arthur.

Not all the places described in this guide are historic; some are not even old. But all are unique. Some are filled with one-of-a-kind antiques, many feature stunning gardens, a few have resident ghosts, and one even keeps Clydesdale draught horses on the property.

Breathtaking scenery, fascinating history, unexplored wilderness, limitless outdoor activities and a sense of being in a place the rest of the world hasn't yet discovered - this is the secret of Tasmania. Most people come to this beautiful island for only a short time and wish they could stay forever. We know. We did. We do.

Tasmania is truly Australia's best kept secret.

HOW TO USE THIS BOOK

Here are some quick hints and explanations to help you get the most out of this book.

Cities, towns and villages are listed in alphabetical order and are also shown on the map at the front of the book. An index listing accommodation alphabetically is found at the back of the book.

Accommodation may be booked directly with the contact person listed in the guide, or bookings may be arranged through the Tasmanian Tourist Office in your city. Some places require deposits; many do not accept credit cards. Prices quoted are based on current research and may vary slightly; EAP means 'Each Additional Person'.

Book early to avoid disappointment. Holidays are often booked well in advance. This includes boats and flights.

Booking addresses are often different from the actual location of the accommodation. When there is a difference, both are noted.

Don't judge your driving time by the map. Many roads are narrow and winding and will require more time than you would expect.

'Exclusively Yours' means just that—the accommodation is exclusively yours for the length of your stay with no sharing of rooms or facilities.

Rates given are in Australian dollars and are subject to change without notice.

Some smaller towns have a limited selection of eating establishments that may only be open for a few hours in the evening. Be prepared!

Don't judge the size of a town by its size on the map. Many towns that appear to be large are actually quite small and may not have petrol stations, banks, etc. There are no banks in the Port Arthur area so you may want to stop at one before you get there.

Continental breakfast *usually* includes cereal, fruit juices, toast or other baked goods, and tea or coffee.

A note to the handicapped: unfortunately, many of the places listed in this guide are not readily accessible to wheelchairs. In most cases this is due to the age and design of the building. Bathtubs are available in many, but not all. If you require one, please inquire when booking. We have attempted to be as accurate as possible in our assessments, which are as follows:

- Minimal assistance: one or two steps at entrance.
- Some assistance: more than two steps, but still relatively accessible.
- Not recommended: access possible, but difficult.
- No access: all rooms on second floor, or narrow doors and hallways prevent access.

REF. NO.	CITY/PLACE NAME	REF. NO.	CITY/PLACE NAME
1	Brighton	15	Middleton
2	Carrick	16	New Norfolk
3	Chudleigh	17	Nile
4	Deloraine	18	Oatlands
5	Devonport	19	Orford
6	Evandale	20	Pioneer
7	Frankford	21	Port Arthur (Koonya, Taranna)
8	Hamilton	22	Richmond
9	Hobart (Bellerive, Lindisfarne, Battery Point)	23	Rosevears
10	Kayena	24	Ross
11	Kempton	25	Stanley (Black River, Wiltshire)
12	Lalla-Lilydale	26	Strahan
13	Launceston	27	Swansea (Lisdillon Estate)
14	Longford	28	Ulverstone
		29	Westbury

LISTING OF ACCOMMODATION BY LOCATION

Page No.

THE COTTAGE
(exclusively yours)
circa 1835
Briggs Road, Brighton, 25 minutes north of Hobart

On the original deed for the property on which The Cottage stands, the old road along the Jordan River is called 'Pensioner's Row'. Military personnel supervising convicts constructing the nearby Bridgewater causeway were granted a plot of land and a stone cottage upon completion of the project in the 1830s.

After building their Bonorong Wildlife Park, Barbara and Ken Jones purchased the tumbledown colonial house on a neighboring property and faithfully renovated it. For the last three years they have rented it out as a haven for honeymooners and others looking for an intimate escape.

City dwellers will delight in the tranquillity of the scene, where the only sounds are from the birds and neighboring livestock. Constructed from sandstone with convict labor, the cottage is surrounded by a lovely garden and stands at the crest of a hill overlooking the Jordan River. The front verandah is an ideal place to contemplate this scene while enjoying your morning tea or planning day trips to the historic Midlands area or perhaps into Hobart.

The interior of the cottage is furnished in a comfortable colonial style, with a sprinkling of antiques and interesting period pieces. A modern kitchen and bathroom provide creature comforts. Two bedrooms (one twin, one double) and a cosy sitting room complete with wood burning fireplace complete the accommodation.

Visitors should not miss a visit to Bonorong Park to see very healthy and tame wombats, kangaroos, rosellas, and other native animals. Be sure to ask Barbara what time she plans to feed the Tasmanian devils—they put on quite a show!

CONTACT: Barbara & Ken Jones

PHONE: (002) 68 1184

BOOKING ADDRESS:
Bonorong Wildlife Center
The Cottage
Briggs Road
Brighton, Tasmania 7030

PRICES: $60 Double
** $12 EAP**

CREDIT CARDS: None

BREAKFAST: Ingredients for a full
cooked breakfast included

FACILITIES: Private

HANDICAPPED: Not recommended
for wheelchairs

PETS: Permitted with prior approval

OTHER: Heaters, full kitchen
facilities, parking, BBQ in garden,
laundry available, no phone on
premises.

HAWTHORN VILLA

circa 1875

Carrick, 18 km west of Launceston

This stately Victorian home set in two acres of beautiful English gardens is a landmark in the historic town of Carrick. The house was built by local miller and archdeacon T. W. Monds in 1875; the garden features two giant California Redwood trees imported and planted by him over one hundred years ago.

Helen Castillo, who recently became a proud Australian citizen, describes Hawthorn Villa as a 'friendly home' and this feeling begins the moment you step inside. Fresh flowers, log fires and antique furnishings add to the Victorian ambience of this charming place.

Hearty cooked breakfasts are served in a sunny dining room on crisp white linen tablecloths with delicate china and elegant sterling place settings. This attention to detail is carried through to the five inviting bedrooms and guest sitting room, which offers a collection of antique typewriters and a selection of books and games.

On the weekends, Helen serves morning and afternoon teas consisting of a three-tiered platter of finger sandwiches, fruit scones and dainty cakes. There is also a variety of homemade jams and marmalade available for sale in country-style jars.

Although minutes from Launceston, the pretty countryside surroundings of Hawthorn Villa will make you feel as if you're a hundred kilometres away.

CONTACT: Helen Castillo

PHONE: (003) 93 6150

BOOKING ADDRESS:
Hawthorn Villa
Corner Bass Highway and
**   Church Street**
(Bishopsbourne Road)
Carrick, Tasmania 7291

PRICES: $60 Double
** $35 Single**
** $15 EAP**

CREDIT CARDS: VISA, BC

BREAKFAST: Full cooked breakfast
included

FACILITIES: 3 doubles with en suite,
1 double shares with 1 single

HANDICAPPED: No wheelchair
access

PETS: Permitted with prior approval

OTHER: TV/Radio in lounge, heaters,
laundry available, dinner by
arrangement, off-street parking,
phone on premises.

BENTLEY COTTAGE

(exclusively yours)
circa 1879
Chudleigh, 70 km west of Launceston

The main home on historic Bentley Farm was built as a wedding gift in 1879 for a Mr. Norman Cameron. It seems that Mr. Cameron's parents did not want him to marry a wild colonial girl, and bribed him with this house to find a proper wife back in England. He did just that and then returned to live here at Bentley. The external walls of this sturdy home are three bricks thick. A broad verandah with iron trim is still supported by the original pine posts although the rest of the house has undergone extensive renovations.

Guest accommodation is in a separate wing of the house, in an area that was originally a smoking room. The fully self-contained cottage features two twin bedrooms, a spacious kitchen, and a large sitting room with a wood burning stove. Ingredients for a continental breakfast are supplied.

Guests at Bentley today can go for a bushwalk, observe farm activities on this beef cattle and sheep farm, or fish for trout in a well-stocked dam. Eldest son Nick reports the trout average four pounds, but they must be released.

CONTACT: Mrs. V. Cramp

PHONE: (003) 63 6131

BOOKING ADDRESS:
Bentley Farm
Chudleigh, Tasmania 7304

PRICES: $45 Double
          $30 Single
          $10 EAP
Reduced rate for children

CREDIT CARDS: None

BREAKFAST: Ingredients for a
continental breakfast included

FACILITIES: Private

HANDICAPPED: Wheelchair access
with minimal assistance

PETS: Not permitted

OTHER: Radio, heaters, full kitchen
facilities, laundry available, off-street
parking, phone at main house,
maximum stay six nights.

BONNEY'S INN

circa 1828

Deloraine, midway between Launceston and Devonport

Bonney's was built in 1828 as a coaching inn by John Bonney, the son of a convict. Today, Bonney's is primarily a colonial tea room and restaurant, but also offers accommodation. Delicious morning and afternoon teas are served six days a week, featuring freshly baked scones, muffins, and other tempting treats. More substantial meals are also available, including lasagna and homemade steak and kidney pies. Dinner is available by arrangement, but only if six or more are to be served.

Accommodation is available in two rooms (one double, one single) over the actual tea room; a separate self-contained unit that can sleep four is located beside the Inn. The architectural integrity of the Inn was maintained in converting the upstairs to provide accommodation. Both rooms are let as one unit, so no sharing of facilities is required. The two rooms include coffee/tea-making facilities, private bathroom, and a small downstairs sitting room with a fireplace.

Both units are restored and furnished in colonial style, and the Inn stands amid a small English style garden. A continental breakfast is included in the tariff, and is served in the tea room on lace tablecloths and fine china.

CONTACT: Mal & Dave Streeter

PHONE: (003) 62 2974

BOOKING ADDRESS:
Bonney's Inn
17 West Parade
Deloraine, Tasmania 7304

PRICES: Rooms in the Inn:
    $50 Double
    $40 Single
    Holiday Cottage:
    $65 Double
    $50 Single
Deposit Required

CREDIT CARDS: MC, VISA, BC

BREAKFAST: Continental breakfast included

FACILITIES: All private

HANDICAPPED: No wheelchair access

PETS: Not permitted

OTHER: TV in lounge, dinner by arrangement (BYO), laundry available, ample street parking, no phone on premises, closed December 25, 26 and Good Friday. Deposit required.

RIVER VIEW LODGE
circa 1877
Devonport, north-west coast

Ideally located, River View Lodge makes a delightful home base from which to visit many interesting places in and around Devonport. Day tours in the area include Cradle Mountain, Mole Creek Wildlife Parks and Caves, Mt. Roland, Boat Harbour and many others.

As the name implies, the River View Lodge has a lovely view of the River Mersey. The warm breakfast room looks across the river to the original site of Devonport's shipyards, established in 1874 by Captain John Griffith, one of the first settlers of Devonport. Griffith's son, Sydney, eventually took over the business and built River View Lodge as his private residence. One of the ships built in this shipyard was the brig *Waverley*, now depicted on the Australian $5 note.

The River View Lodge has eight very spacious rooms all with country style decor and bright atmosphere. There are two single rooms and six doubles, three of which can accommodate a small family. A cosy lounge with an open fire is the perfect place to relax or start a good book. Breakfast is served in the dining room and after one of Rita's delicious breakfasts you won't be needing lunch!

CONTACT: Bruce & Rita Sharman

PHONE: (004) 24 7357

BOOKING ADDRESS:
River View Lodge
Devonport, Tasmania 7310

PRICES: $46 Double with
   en suite, $36 without
             $36 Single with
   en suite, $26 without
             $10 EAP
Reduced rate for children

CREDIT CARDS: None

BREAKFAST: Full cooked breakfast
included

FACILITIES: Some rooms have en
suites, others have shared facilities

HANDICAPPED: Wheelchair access
with minimal assistance

PETS: Not permitted

OTHER: TV in lounge, heaters ($3
rental charge), laundry available, off-
street parking, gold phone on
premises.

SOLOMON COTTAGE

(exclusively yours)
circa 1838
Evandale, 15 minutes from Launceston

Solomon Cottage is an ideal haven for honeymooners or those seeking a quiet escape. The cottage was originally built as a bakehouse for the general store, which is now a lovely tea room known as Solomon House.

The last loaf of bread was baked in 1960 and the bakehouse was used as a storage shed until the present owners completed its restoration in 1985.

The most unique feature of the cottage is the old oven which is now an elevated bedroom featuring a stunning mahogany half-tester bed. The bedroom overlooks a cosy sitting room with a wood burning fireplace and views across the Western Tiers. A door off the sitting room leads to a twin bedroom.

The cottage is furnished in colonial style with fine antiques such as an old pedal organ, a classic seaman's chest and even an oven paddle once used in the bakehouse. A continental breakfast is served

in the sunlit conservatory of the cottage and a cooked breakfast is
available upon request. Dinner is also available by arrangement.

<table>
<tr><td>

CONTACT: Jane Maxwell

PHONE: (003) 91 8331

BOOKING ADDRESS:
Solomon Cottage
1 High Street
Evandale, Tasmania 7212

PRICES: $65 Double
           $45 Single
           $15 EAP
Reduced rate for children

CREDIT CARDS: None

BREAKFAST: Ingredients for a
continental breakfast included

</td><td>

FACILITIES: Private

HANDICAPPED: Wheelchair access
with some assistance

PETS: Not permitted

OTHER: TV available if required,
heaters, tea/coffee-making facilities,
refrigerators, laundry available, BBQ,
dinner by arrangement, off-street
parking, phone available next door.

</td></tr>
</table>

FERNHILL HOST FARM
circa 1880
Frankford, 40 minutes from Launceston or Devonport

Fernhill Host Farm is set in the heart of 280 acres of picturesque farmland and rainforest. Squabbling turkeys and chooks gather on the narrow unsealed driveway that climbs up to this handsomely restored Victorian farmhouse. Built in 1880, Fernhill was used as a private residence until the 1930s when it was abandoned and began a fifty year period of neglect. It took six years of dedication for the present owners to restore Fernhill to its current alluring state.

The three attic guest rooms (two double, one twin) are furnished with brass and iron bedsteads, classic rocking chairs and handcrafted quilts. The sloped ceilings contribute to the charm of the rooms, together with plenty of windows and flourishing indoor plants. A tasty cooked breakfast is served in the dining room or can be eaten on the balcony overlooking lush hillsides and grazing stock. Dinner is also available by arrangement.

Fernhill Host Farm is located midway between Launceston and Devonport and is close to the scenic Tamar Valley, Baker's Beach National Park and the historic town of Beaconsfield.

CONTACT: Helen & Barry
Ferguson

PHONE: (003) 96 1283

LOCATION:
Holwell Road, Frankford

BOOKING ADDRESS:
Fernhill Host Farm
c/o P.O.
Frankford, Tasmania 7251

PRICES: $45 Double
           $25 Single
           $20 EAP
Reduced rate for children

CREDIT CARDS: None

BREAKFAST: Full cooked breakfast
included

FACILITIES: Shared

HANDICAPPED: No wheelchair
access

PETS: Permitted with prior approval

OTHER: TV in lounge, heaters, tea/
coffee available at all times, laundry
available, dinner by arrangement, off-
street parking, phone available.

EMMA'S, VICTORIA'S, AND GEORGE'S COTTAGES

(exclusively yours)
Circa 1830, 1845, 1845
Hamilton

Three entrancing fairytale cottages built of sandstone by early convicts are set in the heart of the delightful town of Hamilton. Owner/creator Judy Madden describes her passion for collecting antiques as an 'incurable disease.' She has put this affliction to good use in the restoration and furnishing of these gems. Although similar in style, each cottage has its own unique personality.

Emma is the eldest of the three, and is probably the favorite of garden lovers. Set in a delightful English garden bursting with color, Emma shows off her rustic charm with pit-sawn timber floorboards and walls that were once covered in eighteen layers of wallpaper. The interior is decorated in a fantasy of one-of-a kind antiques that invite exploration. Emma has one double bed and two twins and can accommodate five people.

Victoria is fifteen years younger than Emma and equally alluring. Ideal accommodation for a family with a sense of adventure, Victoria can accommodate five in double and twin bedrooms, plus a vintage cradle for baby. Victoria is appointed with period antiques and overflows with unique memorabilia. Vintage clothing is even available to help you get into the mood.

George is a dignified country gentleman dressed in burgundy, a perfect cottage for a most memorable honeymoon (first or second). Classy, fun, and romantic, George is full of old world whimsy and is the ideal setting for a getaway for two.

All cottages feature wood burning fireplaces, lovely gardens, and pet sheep grazing in the back yard. Guest are invited to examine all three when available, and may choose the one that strikes their fancy. Guests have even been known to swap cottages after a few days for a varied experience.

CONTACT: Judy Madden

PHONE: (002) 86 3270

ADDRESS:
Emma's, George's and Victoria's
Cottages
Judy Madden
Hamilton, Tasmania 7140

PRICES: **$50 Double, room only**
        $60 Double, with
        breakfast ingredients
        $12 EAP

CREDIT CARDS: None

BREAKFAST: Ingredients available
at extra charge

FACILITIES: Private

HANDICAPPED: Wheelchair access
to George's and Emma's with
assistance

PETS: Permitted with prior approval

OTHER: Radio, heaters, full kitchen
facilities, parking, maximum three
night stay during holiday season,
nearest telephone down street.

OVER-THE-BACK

(exclusively yours)
circa 1984
3 km from Hamilton

When you stay at this secluded cottage on the farm of John and Sue Parsons, you'll think you've left the city far behind. A popular weekend retreat for weary citizens of Hobart this cottage, constructed of Tasmanian-grown Radiata Pine, is actually only 3 km down a dirt road off Highway A10 on the outskirts of Hamilton.

The Parsons built this inviting retreat for their retirement home, but in the meantime they let it out to grateful guests who can bushwalk, enjoy water sports, observe farm activities, or just relax. Perched on a rocky hillside overlooking Lake Meadowbank, the cottage is surrounded by native blackwood, wattles, and eucalypts. Sheep and cattle graze contentedly in the surrounding paddocks, and native fauna sighted included kookaburras, wombats, colorful rosellas, and an occasional Tasmanian Devil.

An added attraction is the boathouse at the lakeside. Guests have access to a rowboat for trout fishing or a windsurfer if they are game. The boatshed contains all the necessities for a BBQ or a picnic, and even has fishing gear for rent and a refrigerator to keep the drinks cold! The Parsons have also been known to take some guests water skiing.

The cottage itself is thoroughly modern, panelled inside with warm pine, comfortable country style furnishings, and a wood burning stove. The kitchen is fully equipped, the bathroom contains a shower and bathtub, and full laundry facilities are included.

Over-the-Back is the perfect location for a family holiday or a romantic retreat, with accommodation for up to seven people in one double bedroom, one triple, and two cots. Book early though—weekends and holidays are usually reserved well in advance.

<table>
<tr><td>

CONTACT: John & Sue Parsons

PHONE: (002) 86 3230 or 86 3276

BOOKING ADDRESS:
Over-the-Back
P.O. Box 35
Hamilton, Tasmania 7140

PRICES: $50 Double
** $15 EAP**
Reduced rate for children

CREDIT CARDS: None

BREAKFAST: Ingredients available
on request

</td><td>

FACILITIES: Private

HANDICAPPED: Designed for
wheelchair access

PETS: Not permitted

OTHER: TV, radio, heaters, full
kitchen facilities, laundry, fishing,
windsurfer, rowboat, water skiing by
arrangement. Phone at main house, 3
km away. Minimum stay 2 nights on
weekends and school holidays, 3 nights
on long weekends, and 4 nights at
Easter. NO FIREARMS, PLEASE.

</td></tr>
</table>

THE OLD SCHOOLHOUSE

circa 1856
Hamilton

Convict stonemasons took two years to complete this massive two-storey stone structure. This historic schoolhouse began admitting children in 1858. Originally, it was a one-room schoolhouse, with quarters for the headmaster upstairs. Boys and girls entered from separate entrances on opposite sides of the building.

With eventual deterioration after decades of use, the old schoolhouse was replaced by a newer facility. In 1972 the structure was condemned and about to be demolished, but local citizens rallied together and raised enough money to save the schoolhouse and begin restoration. Since that time it has served as a private residence for several owners, and is presently in the caring hands of Marilyn and John Yerbury.

Two guest bedrooms and a cosy sitting room are on the ground floor and the Yerbury family lives upstairs in the old schoolmaster's quarters. The spacious rooms feature hardwood floors and antique furniture; fresh flowers add a touch of home.

Built from the remaining sandstone blocks of an old neighborhood brewery, a separate self-contained studio has been built at the back of the home. This studio has a cottagey look, complete with fireplace and antique furnishings. It features private facilities and a private entrance. School was never like this!

CONTACT: Marilyn & John Yerbury

PHONE: (002) 86 3292

BOOKING ADDRESS:
The Old Schoolhouse
Hamilton, Tasmania 7140

PRICES: $45 Double or Studio
          $30 Single
          $15 EAP
Reduced rate for children

CREDIT CARDS: None

BREAKFAST: Full cooked breakfast included
(Ingredients for cooked breakfast supplied to Studio)

FACILITIES: Shared
(Studio has private facilities)

HANDICAPPED: Wheelchair access with some assistance

PETS: Not permitted

OTHER: TV in lounge, heaters, tea/coffee available at all times, laundry available, off-street parking, dinner by arrangement, phone on premises.

BARTON COTTAGE

circa 1837
Battery Point, Hobart

Barton Cottage is located on a quiet residential street at historic Battery Point, only a two-minute walk from the city. Some of the bricks used to build Barton Cottage came to Tasmania from England as ballast on a sailing ship. Built in 1837 by Captain William Wilson, a merchant who arrived in Tasmania on the *Deveron* in the 1820s, this charming cottage has an early colonial atmosphere while offering modern accommodation.

There are three rooms downstairs which include the Guest Room, the Master's Bedroom, and conveniently located across the hall, the Mistress' Bedroom. All three are large, spacious doubles and the latter two are also equipped with an additional single.

Upstairs you will find the Butler and Housemaid's Quarters, the Footman and Pantrymaid's Room and the Chambermaid's Bedchambers. These attic rooms are bright and airy with sloped ceilings and plenty of windows.

All the rooms have private facilities and are decorated with antiques and other old world furnishings to recreate the charm of Hobart's early colonial life. The cottage is open to the public in the afternoons for Devonshire tea.

CONTACT: Sue Sawbridge

PHONE: (002) 23 6808

BOOKING ADDRESS:
Barton Cottage
72 Hampden Road, Battery Point
Hobart, Tasmania 7000

PRICES: $60 Double
          $45 Single
          $15 EAP
Reduced rate for children under 5

CREDIT CARDS: None

BREAKFAST: Full cooked breakfast included

FACILITIES: All private

HANDICAPPED: Wheelchair access with minimal assistance

PETS: Not permitted

OTHER: TV, radio, heaters, tea/coffee-making facilities, refrigerators, parking, gold phone on premises.

COLVILLE COTTAGE
circa 1877
Battery Point, Hobart

This pleasant guest house on a narrow street at Battery Point stands behind a white picket fence amidst a fragrant garden thick with roses, geraniums, daphne, and a handful of fruit trees. The cool verandah trimmed with lacy iron fretwork is a perfect spot to enjoy a 'cuppa' after a day of browsing through the antique shops, restaurants, and historic buildings of Battery Point.

The antique furniture of six double rooms (three with an extra single bed, cots available) is accented by fresh flowers and hardwood floors. Each room is unique; some feature an iron four-poster canopy bed and bay window overlooking the garden. All have private en suites. Other interesting architectural features include marble or carved wooden fireplaces, stained glass windows, and wooden doors.

A generous cooked breakfast is served daily in a comfortable dining room. Owner Rosemary Lewis prides herself on friendly service and individual care. She can even arrange baby-sitting for parents who need an evening to themselves.

CONTACT: Rosemary Lewis

PHONE: (002) 23 6968

BOOKING ADDRESS:
Colville Cottage
32 Mona Street, Battery Point
Hobart, Tasmania 7000

PRICES: $58 Double
$45 Single
$13 EAP
Reduced rate for children

CREDIT CARDS: MC, VISA, BC

BREAKFAST: Full cooked breakfast
included

FACILITIES: All private

HANDICAPPED: No wheelchair
access

PETS: Not permitted

OTHER: TV, heaters, tea/coffee-
making facilities, laundry available,
limited off-street parking, baby-sitting
available by prior arrangement, gold
phone on premises.

COVE COTTAGE PENTHOUSE

(exclusively yours)
circa 1847
Central Hobart

A touch of colonial charm with all the modern conveniences of today, this opulent penthouse is situated above an antique shop on the Hobart waterfront overlooking the Parliament House and its lovely gardens.

The Penthouse crowns a structure built in 1847 as the Sailor's Delight Inn, and is ideally located for taking in the sights of the city. The Salamanca Place Market is a two-minute walk away and there are several licensed restaurants within half a block. Cove Cottage Penthouse also has its own fully equipped kitchen and the refrigerator is usually stocked with a few goodies.

The two double rooms and one twin room are furnished in colonial style with period antiques and can accommodate seven adults. The large bathroom is complete with a claw-footed bathtub and separate shower.

A small solarium is entered through the kitchen, and is a good spot to enjoy a glass of wine while watching the sun set behind the mountains.

Cove Cottage Penthouse offers short to longer term stays; reduced rates are available for longer bookings. A minimum stay of two nights is required.

<table>
<tr><td>

CONTACT: Rick & Barbara Reynolds

PHONE: (002) 23 3553 or 28 1964 (A.H.)

LOCATION:
7 Murray Street, Hobart

BOOKING ADDRESS:
Cove Cottage Penthouse
c/- Hobart Antiques
59 Salamanca Place
Hobart, Tasmania 7000

PRICES: $95 Double
** $10 EAP**

CREDIT CARDS: MC, VISA, BC

BREAKFAST: Not included

</td><td>

FACILITIES: Private

HANDICAPPED: No wheelchair access

PETS: Not permitted

OTHER: Remote control TV, radio, heaters, full kitchen facilities, full laundry, intercom system to entrance, direct dial phone, two-night minimum stay. Metered parking on street, but there is a reserved space for the penthouse a two-minute walk away. Special rates for longer stays.

</td></tr>
</table>

CROMWELL COTTAGE
circa 1880
Battery Point, Hobart

Conveniently located in historic Battery Point, Cromwell Cottage is minutes from the city centre and within walking distance of lovely antique shops, historic buildings and first class restaurants.

This two-storey bed and breakfast sits on a hill overlooking the Derwent River. Each room is uniquely decorated and includes private facilities. A large English breakfast is served daily in a comfortable dining room or can be taken in your room on request.

The Garden Room is on the ground floor and features a double brass bed and chandeliers. The Red Room (only if you really like the color red) is also on the ground floor and has three single beds. The Blue and Yellow Rooms are attic rooms with lovely river views and sloped ceilings. The Blue Room is suitable for a family, with double and twin bedrooms. The Yellow Room is a sunny room with double and single beds in one bedroom.

CONTACT: Janet French

PHONE: (002) 23 6734

BOOKING ADDRESS:
Cromwell Cottage
6 Cromwell Street, Battery Point
Hobart, Tasmania 7000

PRICES: $58 Double
          $45 Single
          $13 EAP
Reduced rate for children

CREDIT CARDS: VISA, BC

BREAKFAST: Full cooked breakfast
included

FACILITIES: All private

HANDICAPPED: No wheelchair
access

PETS: Not permitted

OTHER: TV, radio, heaters, tea/
coffee-making facilities, laundry
available, limited off-street parking,
phone available.

HOLM LODGE
circa 1880
Bellerive, 15 minutes from Hobart

Located in the historic area of Bellerive, on the eastern shore of the Derwent, Holm Lodge is a stone's throw from a peaceful beach and affords beautiful views of Hobart and Mount Wellington. The main house is of historic interest and the Cooper family has recently added a guest lodge which blends perfectly with the colonial architecture of their home.

Guests are more than welcome to join family functions in the main house or, if they prefer, can enjoy the privacy of their suite. The lodge has three rooms, each with its own private entrance and private facilities. There are two twin rooms and one double room with an extra single bed. The rooms are attractively decorated and guests are often surprised to find fruits, homemade chocolates, or other goodies awaiting their arrival.

A large continental breakfast is served in the house and consists of croissants, rolls, toast, homemade jams or marmalade, cheeses and stewed fruit. Dinner is available by arrangement, and highly recommended!

**CONTACT: Desmond & Miriam
Cooper**

PHONE: (002) 44 3656

BOOKING ADDRESS:
Holm Cottage
24 Victoria Esplanade
Bellerive, Hobart 7018

PRICES: $48 Double
** $33 Single**
** $18 EAP**
Reduced rate for children

CREDIT CARDS: None

**BREAKFAST: Large continental
breakfast included**

FACILITIES: All private

HANDICAPPED:
**Wheelchair access with minimal
assistance**

PETS: Not permitted

**OTHER: TV in lounge, heaters, tea/
coffee-making facilities, laundry
available, off-street parking, dinner by
arrangement, phone available.**

ISLINGTON ELEGANT PRIVATE HOTEL
circa 1845
South Hobart

Designed for the up-market traveller who prefers personalised attention to the anonymity of an international hotel, the Islington is set in one and a half acres of a quiet residential area of Hobart, offering breathtaking views of Mt. Wellington. Serving as a posh school upon its completion in 1845, the Islington was later purchased as a private residence and has changed hands several times since.

The spacious entrance hall with its elegant tiles, high ceilings and picture-perfect flower arrangements is just a taste of the extra special attention for which Islington is famous. Eight elegant rooms are furnished with an emphasis on comfort, high quality, and regard for detail. Several of the suites offer direct access to the lovely gardens, which feature roses in the same apricot color as the exterior of the house. Guests can relax with a drink and a good book in the shade of a willow tree, or stroll round the lush grounds. For the more energetic guest, a swimming pool and tennis court are available. Islington also provides a tranquil setting for garden tea parties and other small functions.

A full continental breakfast is served in the windowed conservatory which offers impressive views of the garden and distant mountain peaks. Freshly squeezed orange juice, wholemeal and sultana breads, fresh croissants, and homemade jams and marmalade await you each morning at your leisure.

Service and elegance are the keynotes of Islington, and the little things are not overlooked. A host or hostess is always available for a fresh cuppa, to book a tour or restaurant, or even drive you to dinner if you wish.

CONTACT: Hayden & Judith Oxley

PHONE: (002) 23 3900 or 23 7911

BOOKING ADDRESS:
Islington Elegant Private Hotel
321 Davey Street
Hobart, Tasmania 7000

PRICES: $95 Grand room
** $85 Double**
** $65 Single**
Children not encouraged

CREDIT CARDS: MC, VISA,
AMEX, DC, BC

BREAKFAST: Continental breakfast
included

FACILITIES: All private

HANDICAPPED: Wheelchair access
with minimal assistance

PETS: Not permitted

OTHER: TV in lounge, radios,
heaters, tea/coffee available at all
times, off-street parking, STD/ISD
phones.

ORANA

circa 1909
Lindisfarne, eastern shore, 6 minutes from Hobart

Orana is a beautifully restored Edwardian home at Lindisfarne on the eastern shore of the River Derwent. Situated on a spacious corner lot and surrounded by a large garden that still contains the original horse and buggy circle, Orana offers a magnificent view of the Derwent and the Tasman Bridge.

Orana was built as a holiday retreat by Ellen Pearce, widow of John Pearce, a respected Hobart businessman. Pearce was the son of a transported convict who later became a shipowner, merchant, and member of the Hobart City Council. Ellen, reputedly the owner of the first automobile on the eastern shore, lived at Orana until her death in 1942 at 92 years of age.

In subsequent years, the house was a private residence, a home for boys, and a half-way house. Claire and Brian Marshall began their transformation of Orana in 1983. A detailed historical account and photographic record of the restoration process is on display in the comfortable guest sitting room.

The name Orana is an aboriginal term meaning 'Welcome'. Guests are certainly made to feel welcome at Orana, beginning with the fresh fruit, sweets and cider in the room upon arrival. A large and varied cooked breakfast is served in the dining area. Tea and coffee are always available, and there are usually some freshly baked goodies to tempt you. Hot scones, a chocolate cake, or apple muffins are a welcome surprise for an afternoon or late night snack. You'll consider forgoing your sightseeing to wait around the house to see what will come out of the oven next.

The four guest rooms are graciously furnished with antiques and memorabilia of the period. The many little extras and personal service at Orana combine with the elegant surroundings to make your stay memorable.

<table>
<tr><td>

CONTACT: Claire & Brian Marshall

PHONE: (002) 43 9017

BOOKING ADDRESS:
Orana
20 Lowelly Road
Lindisfarne, Tasmania 7015
PRICES: $50 Double
          $35 Single
          $15 EAP
Reduced rate for children
Special—stay 7 nights and only pay for 5!

CREDIT CARDS: MC, BC

BREAKFAST: Full cooked breakfast included

</td><td>

FACILITIES: All private

HANDICAPPED: Wheelchairs not recommended

PETS: Not permitted

OTHER: TV in lounge, radio, heaters, tea/coffee available at all times, laundry available, parking, phone available, baby-sitting may be available by prior arrangement.

</td></tr>
</table>

TANTALLON LODGE
circa 1906
Battery Point, Hobart

An imposing two-storey brick structure in the heart of Battery Point, Tantallon Lodge stands on a hillside with glorious views of the Derwent and surrounding mountains. Tantallon once served as a boarding house, but has been extensively renovated and now can accommodate up to seventeen guests in elegant style.

The building contains many architecturally interesting details, including stained glass, carved blackwood mantelpieces, window awnings, and an octagonal-shaped tower on one corner. The seven guest rooms are spacious and airy; all are handsomely decorated in period furniture. Some rooms include incredible panoramic views and one has its own verandah.

The stately dining room is well appointed with a fireplace, lacy chandeliers, dark wooden dining tables, and crisp linen tablecloths. A full cooked breakfast is included in the tariff, and tea/coffee facilities are available in all rooms.

CONTACT: Rhona & Ted Moule

PHONE: (002) 23 3124

BOOKING ADDRESS:
Tantallon Lodge
8 Mona Street, Battery Point
Hobart, Tasmania 7000

PRICES: $60 Double
          $45 Single
          $15 EAP
Reduced rate for children

CREDIT CARDS: None

BREAKFAST: Full cooked breakfast
included

FACILITIES: All private

HANDICAPPED: Wheelchair access
with some assistance

PETS: Not permitted

OTHER: TV, radios, heaters, tea/
coffee-making facilities, refrigerators,
limited off-street parking, gold phone
on premises.

WARWICK COTTAGES

(exclusively yours)
circa 1854
Old Hobart Town, 1 km from G.P.O.

These precious convict-built brick cottages in Old Hobart Town offer unique accommodation in a colonial atmosphere. Standing side by side, 'Annie's Room' and 'Pandora's Box' are identical in structure but each has its own special charm and character. Both cottages sleep four with two single beds downstairs; a delightful winding staircase leads to a double room in each attic.

The cottages were built by Henry Howard, a convict, who was granted his ticket of leave in 1851, and his conditional pardon three years later. In 1853, he was married to Hanna Brain at Battery Point. Their first child was born in Annie's Room in 1855 and their seventh twelve years later.

Annie's Room and Pandora's Box are snug romantic cottages with a special warmth and a feeling of yesteryear. Both are self-contained units which have been beautifully restored in a colonial style. The kitchens are fully equipped with all the ingredients necessary for a cooked breakfast and the shelves are filled with unusual antique bric-a-brac. In each sitting room, you will find an old weather-beaten wooden chest, perhaps used by seamen in the early whaling days. Pandora's kitchen is decorated with old-fashioned carriage lanterns and even has a vintage meat grinder.

<table>
<tr><td>

CONTACT: Lyne Agnew

PHONE: (002) 54 1264

LOCATION:
119-121 Warwick Street, Hobart

BOOKING ADDRESS:
Waverley Cottages
Oatlands, Tasmania, 7120

PRICES: $80 Double
$70 Single
$20 EAP

CREDIT CARDS: VISA, BC

BREAKFAST: Ingredients for a
cooked breakfast included

</td><td>

FACILITIES: Private

HANDICAPPED: No wheelchair
access

PETS: Not permitted

OTHER: TV in lounge, radio, heaters,
full kitchen facilities, laundry
available, street parking, no phone on
premises.

</td></tr>
</table>

ORPLID VEGETARIAN HOST FARM

circa 1981

Kayena, 39 km north of Launceston

Born in Germany and citizens of Sweden, Inge and Helmut Gehrmann arrived in Tasmania in 1981 and have built their snug little organic farm into a showcase of alternative lifestyles. More than forty kinds of vegetables are grown at Orplid, (German for 'The Place of my Dreams') along with numerous flowers, herbs, and fruits. Inge is proud of the fact that she can serve guests homegrown vegetables 365 days a year, and also supply vegies to several first class restaurants in Launceston.

Accommodation is spartan but comfortable, but luxury is not why guests come to Orplid. Guests have the opportunity to learn the rudiments of a wholistic lifestyle, or can explore a broad range of subjects in Orplid's book and cassette tape library. The hundreds of books include such titles as *Pyramid Power*, *How to Enjoy Your Weeds*, and *A Course in Miracles*. Several works (in German) by Albert Schweitzer are also on the shelves. Cassette tapes range from *Possibility Thinking*, *Meditation*, and *The Healing Power of Humor* to the intimidating *Transpersonal Psychology and Psychosynthesis*.

Inge's main passion is gardening, but she also teaches popular vegetarian cooking classes. If you plan to stay at Orplid, be sure to book in advance and don't miss having a delicious vegetarian meal prepared by Inge. We are not vegetarians, but thoroughly enjoyed a three-course dinner featuring a selection of delicious salads, soy pasta with mushroom and onion sauce, celeriac, and homemade peppermint/apple tea. Breakfast was an unusually tasty triticale porridge (a grain that is a cross between wheat and rye and was developed in Australia) with dates and raisins and a selection of fruits and jams.

Whether or not you are a vegetarian, Orplid is an interesting experience and Inge's hospitality is warm and genuine.

CONTACT: Inge Gehrmann

PHONE: (003) 94 7174

BOOKING ADDRESS:
Orplid Vegetarian Host Farm
RSD 336
Beaconsfield, Tasmania 7270

PRICES: $50 Double
** $28 Single**
Reduced rate for children

CREDIT CARDS: None

BREAKFAST: Cooked breakfast
included (meatless)

FACILITIES: Communal

HANDICAPPED: Not recommended, but one downstairs room is available. (Breakfast can be served in it.)

PETS: Permitted in downstairs room with prior approval

OTHER:Heaters available on request, (no electric blankets), herbal tea always available, off-street parking, book and tape library. English, Swedish and German spoken. Vegetarian dinners by arrangement (1 day's notice required), vegetarian cooking classes, phone on premises, closed June and July. NO ALCOHOL OR SMOKING, PLEASE.

WILMOT ARMS INN
circa 1844
Kempton, Midlands, 45 km north of Hobart

Built by convicts in 1844, Wilmot Arms Inn served as a licensed coaching inn until 1897, when the proprietor found religion, ceased distilling spirits and fed the remaining 'demon rum' to his pigs! Since that time, the inn has served primarily as a private residence, and was later abandoned and derelict until 1978. Now faithfully restored to its former glory, the Wilmot Arms Inn once again welcomes the traveller with colonial accommodation in an historic atmosphere.

The five rooms (four double and one twin) are simply decorated with delicate antique pieces, and fresh fruit and flowers on bedside tables greet you upon arrival. Enjoy an open fire in the snug sitting room, where you can play a tune on a vintage piano, admire the striking 1884 grandfather clock or examine a collection of early colonial clothing irons.

A large cooked breakfast is served in the quaint dining room and then there is plenty of time to do some sightseeing before Ray and Pamela serve a delightful lunch in their pleasant Old English garden.

CONTACT: Ray & Pamela Norman

PHONE: (002) 59 1272

LOCATION:
Main Road, Kempton

BOOKING ADDRESS:
Wilmot Arms Inn
P.O. Box 93
Kempton, Tasmania 7030

PRICES: $50 Double
$35 Single
$15 EAP
Reduced rate for children

CREDIT CARDS: VISA, BC

BREAKFAST: Full cooked breakfast
included

FACILITIES: Shared

HANDICAPPED: Wheelchair can be
accommodated with prior notice

PETS: Not permitted

OTHER: Heaters, some rooms with
antique radios, tea/coffee available at
all times, dinner by arrangement,
laundry available, parking, phone
available.

PLOVERS RIDGE HOST FARM

circa 1987
Lilydale, 25 km north of Launceston

A country refuge with an abundance of peace and quiet, Plovers Ridge offers breathtaking views of the beautiful Lilydale valley and Mount Arthur. Two independent units (one self-contained) are bright and spacious with plenty of windows allowing you to enjoy the landscape even while you relax inside next to the pot belly stove.

One double room offers full kitchen facilities and its own private terrace with a BBQ. Decorated in modern country furnishings, the room has slate floors, warm wood panelling, and pine furniture. Live plants are placed throughout the unit giving it an extra homey feel.

The other unit has a double bed with two bunks which conveniently fold up to the wall and are hardly noticed. Limited kitchen facilities are available and a meatless cooked breakfast, including homemade breads and yogurts, is served to you in your room. Both units are similarly furnished and both enjoy lovely views. A twin room in the main house is available for larger families or groups needing additional space.

Plovers Ridge is conveniently located for fishing and bushwalking and is only a short drive from the Lavender Farm and Rhododendron Reserve.

<table>
<tr><td>

CONTACT: Colin & Carol Cook

PHONE: (003) 95 1102

BOOKING ADDRESS:
Plovers Ridge Host Farm
Lalla Road
Lilydale, Tasmania 7268

PRICES: **$60 Double**
$38 Single
$17-27 EAP
Reduced rate for children, special family rates
Discount for longer stays

CREDIT CARDS: None

BREAKFAST: Cooked breakfast included (meatless)

</td><td>

FACILITIES: Private

HANDICAPPED: Not recommended

PETS: Permitted with prior approval

OTHER: TV, heaters, tea/coffee-making facilities, refrigerator, laundry available, fireplaces, phone on premises.

</td></tr>
</table>

THE PEAR WALK COTTAGES

(exclusively yours)
circa 1987
Lalla, 25 minutes north-east of Launceston

The Pear Walk takes its name from an historic 500 foot long country lane framed by trellised pear trees and thick plantings of rhododendrons and azaleas. This spectacular spring display has been featured in *Australian House and Garden Magazine*; in earlier days it graced the cover of *The Weekly Courier's* issue of May 8, 1913. The pears blossom in early October, the azaleas and rhododendrons in November.

Although The Pear Walk gives this rural retreat it's name, it is by no means the only attraction. Owner Bruce Goodsir is an architect and artist, bottles his own pear wine, and even raises Clydesdale draught horses on the property! He can sometimes be coaxed into hitching up these magnificent beasts and taking guests for a ride in a colorful wagon or sled.

Accommodation is in two comfortable, self-contained cottages. In addition to the nearby Pear Walk, the cottages are surrounded by bright, well-tended gardens and are close to glass-houses planted with herbs. Gardening enthusiasts will not want to miss the historic rhododendron gardens of Lalla or the Lavender Farm a short drive away.

The cottages themselves are much roomier than they appear from the outside and are attractively finished in light wood tones and soft colors. One cottage sleeps four and the other three; both have full kitchens and include ingredients for a full cooked breakfast.

CONTACT: Libby & Bruce Goodsir

PHONE: (003) 95 4226 or 34 1996

BOOKING ADDRESS:
The Pear Walk
Lalla Road
Lalla, Tasmania 7254
PRICES: $60 Double
             $50 Single
             $15 EAP
Reduced rate for children

CREDIT CARDS: MC, VISA, BC

BREAKFAST: Ingredients for a full cooked breakfast included

FACILITIES: Private

HANDICAPPED: Not recommended

PETS: Permitted with prior approval

OTHER: TV, radio, heaters, full kitchen facilities, laundry available, parking, phone available at main house, tennis court.

AIRLIE HOUSE
circa 1835
Launceston, 2 minutes from city centre

With only three guest rooms (plus one single to accommodate a child or mother-in-law when Mum and Dad want a little privacy), personalised service sets the Airlie House apart. Built on land originally granted to Thomas Nightingale in 1830, the rear section of the home was constructed of timber around 1835. Substantial additions utilising convict-made bricks and handmade nails were completed in the 1870s, giving the home its present facade in the middle Victorian style.

Owner Bev Lane has lovingly restored and decorated the home with pretty antiques and modern reproductions in the Victorian style. Rooms feature bay windows and cast-iron fireplaces. A full cooked breakfast featuring hand-cured bacon, free range eggs, and homemade jam is served in the opulent dining room, accented by fresh flowers and old prints of convict days. A comfortable guest lounge is also available, where a cheery fire warms guests in winter.

CONTACT: Bev Lane

PHONE: (003) 34 0304

BOOKING ADDRESS:
Airlie House
163 George Street
Launceston, Tasmania 7250

PRICES: $55 Double
          $40 Single
          $15 EAP
Reduced rate for children

CREDIT CARDS: MC, VISA, BC

BREAKFAST: Full cooked breakfast
included

FACILITIES: All private

HANDICAPPED: Wheelchair access
with some assistance

PETS: Not permitted

OTHER: TV, radio, heaters, tea/
coffee-making facilities, refrigerator,
laundry available, parking, phone on
premises

ALICE'S PLACE

(exclusively yours)
circa 1987 (1840s materials)
Launceston, 2 minutes from city centre

This enchanting fairytale cottage will satisfy the fantasies of the most ardent escapist. Just the cottage Alice might have seen through the looking glass, Alice's Place was constructed from convict-made bricks and old timbers salvaged from three demolished 1840s era buildings.

Lovingly decorated with the whimsical romantic in mind, no detail has been overlooked. The downstairs is an eclectic clutter of comfortable furniture, antique pieces and delightful bric-a-brac. A stag's head peers down from the mantel over the wood burning fireplace; New Guinea turtle shells hang opposite. Every nook and cranny provides a new surprise. Open a desk drawer and find a pair of turn-of-the-century gloves. Play an old phonograph record on the Victrola. Victorian style costumes are even provided to help you get into the mood.

Upstairs, colonial bed steps (concealing a colonial commode) lead to a huge four-poster canopy bed decorated with a handmade quilt and lacy feather pillows. Two single beds are also available in a second bedroom. A tiny balcony overlooks the quaint, English style garden, complete with fresh flowers and herbs that guests are free to use in the fully equipped kitchen. All modern conveniences are well hidden, ingredients for a full breakfast are provided.

Enjoy a soak in the old-fashioned footed bathtub supplied with perfumed bath oils; this brass-fitted bathroom even includes hair dryers!

Owner/designer Helen Poynder once owned an antique and used clothing shop in Launceston. Alice's Place and neighboring Ivy Colonial Cottage are the personification of her collecting impulses. They are not merely accommodation—they are an experience!

<table>
<tr><td>

CONTACT: Helen Poynder

PHONE: (003) 31 8431 or 31 7481

BOOKING ADDRESS:
Alice's Place
17 York Street
Launceston, Tasmania 7250

PRICES: $70-80 Double
     (depending on season)
     $14 EAP

CREDIT CARDS: None

BREAKFAST: Ingredients for a full cooked breakfast included

</td><td>

FACILITIES: Private

HANDICAPPED: No wheelchair access

PETS: Permitted with prior approval

OTHER: TV, radio, full kitchen facilities, laundry available, parking, phone nearby

</td></tr>
</table>

BOATWRIGHT HOUSE
circa 1901
Launceston, 5 minutes from city centre

Restored to its former glory, this brick mansion is a splendid monument to Edwardian elegance. Originally built by the Boatwright family as a private residence, the house served as a girls' boarding school for many years. Wardrobes in some of the rooms still contain evidence of those days, in the form of names and other messages scribbled inside. The house has been a private residence for the last ten years; the present owners admitted their first guests in February of 1988 following extensive restoration and refurnishing.

Tastefully appointed in authentic furnishings from Edwardian times but incorporating modern en suite facilities and appliances, each of the six guest rooms is unique. Brass or iron bedsteads contrast with marble or blackwood mantels and trim. Original cast-iron fireplaces are found throughout, although they are no longer in use.

The sunny dining room is a showcase of antiques sure to delight even the non-enthusiast, highlighted by a turn of the century cash register and fresh cut flowers. No detail has been overlooked, from the dragon gargoyle perched at the peak of the roof to the English garden surrounding the house.

CONTACT: Ian & Sylvia Whitten

PHONE: (003) 34 1579

BOOKING ADDRESS:
Boatwright House
19 Lyttleton Street
Launceston, Tasmania 7250

PRICES: $60 Double
$50 Single
$15 EAP
Reduced rate for children

CREDIT CARDS: MC, VISA,
AMEX, BC

BREAKFAST: Full cooked breakfast
included

FACILITIES: All private

HANDICAPPED: Wheelchair access
to 1 double room with some assistance

PETS: Not permitted

OTHER: TV, radios, heaters, tea/
coffee available at all times, off-street
parking, laundry available, phone
available, picnic baskets/afternoon tea
by arrangement.

HILLVIEW HOUSE
circa 1840
Launceston, 5 minutes from city centre

Hillview House is a central place to call home while taking in the sights of the beautiful city of Launceston. This imposing two-storey white structure laced with green trim stands on a hillside overlooking Launceston and the Tamar River. Built originally to serve as the first grammar school for the children of Launceston, it was later altered and rented out as residential flats. Following extensive renovation, Hillview was converted to a guest house and now serves as a charming retreat for the discerning traveller. Hillview House is only a short stroll away from Launceston's best restaurants and shops.

Each room is individually decorated with a pleasing colonial flair and all have tea/coffee-making facilities and private bathrooms. The dining room has refreshing views of the city and surrounding hillsides. A blazing fire will warm you as you enjoy a delicious cooked breakfast, served with a smile by your hosts, June and Jock Carmichael. The Carmichaels are also happy to suggest touring itineraries and restaurants, and offer individual attention to make you feel at home.

CONTACT: June & Jock
Carmichael

PHONE: (003) 31 7388

BOOKING ADDRESS:
Hillview House
193 George Street
Launceston, Tasmania 7250

PRICES: $49.50 Double
            $39.50 Single
            $10 EAP

CREDIT CARDS: MC, VISA,
AMEX, BC

BREAKFAST: Full cooked breakfast
included

FACILITIES: All private

HANDICAPPED: No wheelchair
access

PETS: Not permitted

OTHER: TV, radio, heaters, tea/
coffee-making facilities, street
parking, gold phone on premises

IVY COTTAGE

(exclusively yours)
circa 1840
Launceston, 2 minutes from city centre

This plain-faced Georgian style cottage with the red roof and white picket fence shares its 17 York Street address with neighboring Alice's Place. Nestled in a charming old-world cottage garden, the interior of the Ivy has undergone a transformation under the loving hands of Helen Poynder.

Furnished in a more faithfully colonial mode than Alice's, Helen's unique style is apparent in many details. An antique bassinet full of precious old stuffed animals beckons from the corner of the kitchen/lounge room. The hallway is wallpapered with dozens of unique old postcards and photographs.

Both bedrooms (one double, one twin) have their own character, with sloped ceilings and Victorian knick-knacks. A small sitting room also contains a wood burning fireplace and an old gramophone. The bathroom sports a footed bathtub and brass fixtures.

The modern kitchen is fully equipped but maintains the colonial feel with old-style pine furniture, stone floor and bric-a-brac. Ingredients for a cooked breakfast (including hand-cured bacon and homemade jams) are supplied. Fresh strawberries and pears grow in the garden. Guests are welcome to pick these fruits or the fresh flowers that grow all around.

At the time of our visit, August '88, Helen was busy creating a third cottage in Launceston—the Camellia Cottage. Built in 1840, this cottage is undergoing extensive refurbishment, and will soon become available for visitors. We look forward to a stay at some future date.

CONTACT: Helen Poynder

PHONE: (003) 31 8431 or 31 7481

BOOKING ADDRESS:
Ivy Cottage
17 York Street
Launceston, Tasmania 7250

PRICES: $68-$74 Double
(depending on season)
** $10-12 EAP**

CREDIT CARDS: None

BREAKFAST: Ingredients for a full
cooked breakfast included

FACILITIES: Private

HANDICAPPED: No wheelchair
access due to narrow hallways

PETS: Permitted with prior approval

OTHER: TV, radio, heaters, full
kitchen facilities, laundry available,
parking, no phone on premises.

KILMARNOCK HOUSE
circa 1905
Launceston, 5 minutes from city centre

Kilmarnock House, an elegant two-storey Edwardian home built in 1905 as a town house for a well-known Launceston merchant, was recently purchased by Bruce and Elizabeth Clark who have lovingly restored it to reflect the splendour and grace of yesteryear.

Antique furnishings and heirlooms are delicately displayed and the luxurious rooms are bright and spacious, each containing a table and chairs. Fresh flowers add a touch of class to all the rooms and common areas. The upstairs hallway provides access to the verandah where, in winter, you can catch a glimpse of snow-capped peaks in the distance.

A continental breakfast, including cereals, fresh orange juice, toast, Tasmanian honey, fruit and teas is provided in each suite. An egg boiler is also available in each room for those who prefer a cooked breakfast.

There are seven beautiful double rooms, one with an additional single bed and one with two sets of bunk beds for a larger family. One of the double rooms has been a favorite for honeymooners because of its romantic decor, highlighted by an antique canopied bed. There are also one twin and one triple room. All rooms have the luxury of an en suite with all facilities.

CONTACT: Bruce & Elizabeth Clark

PHONE: (003) 34 1514 or 44 2175

BOOKING ADDRESS:
Kilmarnock House
66 Elphin Road
Launceston, Tasmania 7250

PRICES: $70 Double
** $55 Single**
** $15 EAP**
Reduced rate for children

CREDIT CARDS: MC, VISA, AMEX, BC

BREAKFAST: Large continental breakfast included

FACILITIES: All private

HANDICAPPED: Wheelchair access with minimal assistance

PETS: Not permitted

OTHER: TV, radio, heaters, limited kitchen facilities, refrigerators, laundry available, off-street parking, gold phone on premises.

MOLECOMBE COTTAGE

(exclusively yours)
circa 1830
10 minutes outside Launceston

Take a drive down a wooded country lane to Molecombe Cottage and you leave modern Launceston seven kilometres and 150 years behind. Arguably the most historically accurate colonial cottage in its restoration and furnishing, Molecombe is a history buff's dream and a honeymooner's fantasy.

When Megan and Bruce England discovered the dilapidated shell that was Molecombe it was suffering from decades of neglect. Three years of painstaking restoration and uncounted hours of hunting for just the right genuine colonial furnishings have resulted in the Molecombe that greets weary travellers today—a magical step back in time.

Hours of stripping off old paint and wallpaper uncovered hand-hewn gum tree floorboards, curved baltic pine ceilings, and intricately carved cedar and pine mantels. One wall in a bedroom at the top of a creaking staircase is a living history book, with remnants of 150 years of paint and wallpaper deliberately left behind during restoration.

Modern day colonists will find new treasures at every turn. Vintage stuffed animals and hand carved duck decoys peer from their perches on huon pine dressing tables. Lacy iron beds stand on colorful rag rugs and are dressed in handmade quilts. The kitchen looks much as it may have in colonial days, with strands of garlic and dried flowers hanging from ceiling timbers and a wood burning stove ready to bake an old fashioned meal. Modern kitchen and bathroom necessities have been artfully incorporated and can easily be overlooked at first glance.

The whitewashed brick and timber structure stands in a tranquil English garden, and overlooks a gently flowing stream and the Launceston Federal Country Club Casino and golf course. Up to seven guests can be accommodated in three bedrooms, two double and one twin.

Molecombe Cottage is now classified by the National Trust and was featured in *Australian House and Gardens' 1986 Yearbook*. Perhaps the most satisfying recognition has come from delighted guests. The guestbook is filled with rapturous praise for this bit of history, lovingly shared by the Englands.

<table>
<tr><td>CONTACT: Megan England</td><td>FACILITIES: Private</td></tr>
<tr><td>PHONE: (003) 31 1355 or 31 7481</td><td>HANDICAPPED: Not recommended for wheelchairs</td></tr>
<tr><td>LOCATION:
Mt. Leslie Road, Launceston</td><td>PETS: Not permitted</td></tr>
<tr><td>BOOKING ADDRESS:
Molecombe Cottage
23 Kenyon Street
Launceston, Tasmania 7250</td><td>OTHER: Heaters, full kitchen facilities, laundry available, fireplaces, parking, no telephone on premises.</td></tr>
<tr><td>PRICES: $65 Double
          $10 EAP</td><td></td></tr>
<tr><td>CREDIT CARDS: None</td><td></td></tr>
<tr><td>BREAKFAST: Ingredients for a full cooked breakfast included</td><td></td></tr>
</table>

THE OLD BAKERY INN

circa 1870
Launceston

The original bakery that occupied this fine old building was started by a Mr. T. Crosby, a deserter from the English Army. Success soon followed and the bakery was chosen to cater the Queen's Jubilee Celebration twenty-seven years later. From then on the bakery was known as the Jubilee Bakery.

Guests entering The Old Bakery today encounter the remains of what was once the main oven, cleverly retained as the centerpiece of the comfortable foyer. Another oven has actually been converted to a guest room, with brick walls two feet thick.

The Old Bakery was restored by Lorna Kelly and Mr. and Mrs. K. Newman, who were also responsible for the restoration of Hillview House. The Old Bakery Inn began charming travellers in 1985, with sixteen individually decorated rooms. Lace curtains, antique furnishings, fresh flowers, and private facilities are standard. Some rooms feature balconies and several overlook a garden courtyard.

Two units are especially unique. The Stable was once the original stables for the horses that delivered the bakery's produce. Located behind the Inn, the Stable is delightfully furnished and offers a bit more privacy. Above the stable is the Loft, a self-contained attic apartment featuring vaulted ceilings, skylights, and views of the neighboring hills and rooftops. A separate self-contained cottage known as the Baker's Cottage is also available nearby.

Breakfast is not included in the tariff, but is served daily in a dining room that in the evening becomes The Folly, a fully licensed restaurant. The Folly is open for dinner seven nights a week and for lunch Monday through Friday. The Menu features innovative cuisine that changes with the seasons, such as sauteed quail in red grape sauce, poached Tasmanian Atlantic salmon with sorrel hollandaise sauce, and a Thai-style seafood bouillabaisse. Numerous publications have praised the Folly; *Gourmet* magazine exclaimed 'Hang the kilojoules, this was nirvana.'

<table>
<tr><td>

CONTACT: Lorna Kelly

PHONE: (003) 31 7900

BOOKING ADDRESS:
The Old Bakery Inn
Corner York and Margaret Streets
Launceston, Tasmania 7250

PRICES: $65 Double
** $53 Single**
**   12 EAP**

CREDIT CARDS: MC, VISA,
AMEX, BC

BREAKFAST: Not included

</td><td>

FACILITIES: All private

HANDICAPPED: Wheelchair access
to ground floor rooms

PETS: Not permitted

OTHER: TV, radios, mini-bars,
refrigerators, tea/coffee-making
facilities, laundry available, limited
off-street parking, STD/ISD phones,
licensed restaurant on premises.

</td></tr>
</table>

BRICKENDON COTTAGE

(exclusively yours)
circa 1830
2 km outside Longford, 20 minutes from Launceston

Located on one of Tasmania's oldest properties, this captivating colonial cottage was originally built to house the coachman and his family. Brickendon Estate has remained in the Archer family since the land was originally granted to William Archer in the 1820s. In addition to the main house and the Coachman's Cottage, several stone buildings and a well known stone chapel of the same vintage still stand on the property behind a tall English hawthorn hedge. The Archers plan additional restorations in coming years.

The Coachman's Cottage is located near the sprawling main house, down a magnificent drive lined with century-old pine and eucalyptus trees. Guests can feel splendidly isolated only minutes from the city. The cottage is a rustic brick structure, fastidiously refurbished in an authentic colonial style.

The interior features the original brick bread oven and several fine pieces of colonial cedar furniture that have been in the family for generations. A weatherboard pine table in a sunlit dining room overlooks a colorful English garden and a nearby lagoon, home to a cacophony of frogs each evening. Other creatures to be heard include flocks of sheep in the surrounding paddocks and cackling kookaburras in the trees.

A creaking wooden staircase leads to two upstairs bedrooms (a double and a twin); the master bedroom houses a quaint hand-hammered tin half bath, complete with a watermark from years of use. Downstairs, another single room opens off of the snug sitting room where guests can enjoy a glass of complimentary port while they contemplate a glowing fire.

The kitchen and bathroon contain all the modern conveniences, unobtrusively installed so the colonial feeling is maintained. Ingredients for a cooked breakfast are included in the tariff and the homemade jam is excellent!

<table>
<tr><td>

CONTACT: Louise Archer

PHONE: (003) 91 1251 or 31 7481

BOOKING ADDRESS:
Brickendon Cottage
P.O. Box 72
Longford, Tasmania 7301

PRICES: **$68 Double**
          $60 Single
          $12 EAP

CREDIT CARDS: None

BREAKFAST: Ingredients for a full
cooked breakfast included

</td><td>

FACILITIES: Private

HANDICAPPED: Wheelchair access
with some assistance

PETS: Allowed with prior approval

OTHER: Radio, heaters, full kitchen
facilities, parking, laundry available,
phone available at main house.

</td></tr>
</table>

HOLLY TREE FARM
circa 1920
Middleton, 50 kms south of Hobart

High on a hillside overlooking the D'Entrecasteaux Channel and rugged Bruny Island, Holly Tree Farm is an excellent example of the late Federation style of architecture. Hosts Wendy and Henry Brigden have lovingly restored and extended the original homestead. Built by a pioneer orchardist in the heart of Tasmania's apple growing region, the home was once completely surrounded by orchards.

Today, Holly Tree Farm is a gardener's delight, with a variety of fruit trees and a myriad of flowers growing in rambling beds. Fresh cut flowers greet guests in each room, even in winter. Eight pet donkeys, sheep, and two pet ducks will entertain guests between bushwalks and day trips to explore this scenic region.

Accommodation is in two spacious modern suites (one twin, one double) furnished with a country-style elegance. Both have en suite facilities and share a separate entrance and a cosy, antique-furnished sitting room with a log fire and enough interesting books to occupy many a winter night. An intimate breakfast for two can be served in the sitting room, complete with farm fresh eggs and homemade jams, served on delicate china and an embroidered lace tablecloth.

A small selection of excellent local crafts is discreetly displayed in the foyer; you will be delighted to learn you may purchase them at prices less than you would expect.

<table>
<tr><td>

CONTACT: Wendy & Henry Brigden

PHONE: (002) 92 1680

BOOKING ADDRESS:
Holly Tree Farm
P.O. Box 23
Middleton, Tasmania 7163

PRICES: $48 Double
** $28 Single**
Reduced rate for children
Discount after two nights stay

CREDIT CARDS: None

BREAKFAST: Full cooked breakfast included

</td><td>

FACILITIES: All private

HANDICAPPED: Wheelchair access with minimal assistance

PETS: Not permitted

OTHER: TV in lounge, radios, heaters, tea/coffee available at all times, guest refrigerator, laundry available, off-street parking, phone available.

</td></tr>
</table>

TYNWALD
WILLOW BEND ESTATE
circa 1830
New Norfolk, 33 km from Hobart on A3

A majestic three-storey structure on a hillside with glorious views of the Derwent River valley, Tynwald is a magnificent monument to Tasmania's colonial heritage. Free settlers John and Martha Terry arrived on a convict ship in 1818 with their eleven children and soon developed a mill and granary on this site. Ruins of this mill still stand adjacent to Tynwald. The property, then known as 'Lachlan River Mill', remained in the family until the depression of the 1890s.

Prominent politician William Moore then purchased the property and renamed it Tynwald, after Tynwald on the Isle of Man. Moore also made the architectural changes that gave Tynwald its present look—the lofty tower, bay windows overlooking a lovely English garden, and wide verandahs on three sides, decorated with lacy iron fretwork.

Tynwald today offers colonial accommodation in six elegantly appointed rooms. Handsome brass and iron beds highlight the spacious guestrooms, which also feature working old radios and a sprinkling of Victorian antiques. The two ground floor rooms feature private facilities; the four upstairs share two bathrooms. Upstairs rooms all have access to the sunny verandah; guests can enjoy the commanding views over a cup of tea. Other amenities include a tennis court and solar heated swimming pool, as well as a gourmet BYO restaurant.

Dinner is available to the public seven nights a week in the Victorian dining room and lunch is served on Sundays. The à la carte menu varies with the seasons, but features fresh local ingredients prepared with a French influence. Samples from a recent menu include a selection of fresh homemade breads, Duckling Melisa (prepared with Malayan spices), and a Seafood Duo consisting of King George whiting and bay bugs with a mango puree and green peppercorns. Be sure to save room for the Salzburg Nockerl, a hot dessert soufflé served with fresh raspberries. House guests have a separate cosy breakfast room, decorated with collected pieces of Victoriana and warmed by an open fire in winter.

CONTACT: Garry Roohan & Patricia Kelsall

PHONE: (002) 61 2667

BOOKING ADDRESS:
Tynwald
Willow Bend Estate,
P.O. Box 51
New Norfolk, Tasmania 7140

PRICES: $68 Double
** $55 Single**
** $20 EAP**
Reduced rate for children

CREDIT CARDS: VISA, BC

BREAKFAST: Full cooked breakfast included

FACILITIES: Some private

HANDICAPPED: Wheelchair access with assistance (one room with en suite is designed especially for wheelchair access)

PETS: Not permitted

OTHER: TV available in lounge, radio, heaters, tea/coffee available at all times, phone available. Jogging track and jet boats nearby, swimming pool, tennis courts. BYO gourmet restaurant on premises.

STRATHMORE COLONIAL ACCOMMODATION

circa 1826

Nile, 30 km south of Launceston

With three hundred serene acres as its setting, convict-built Strathmore is a stunning country estate. Extensive gardens surround the home and a beautiful lake attracts a variety of birdlife. The well-manicured grounds of Strathmore are quickly becoming a popular place for summer weddings and garden parties. An old barn beside the main homestead has been converted to a functions room, with catering for up to 150 people.

Distinctive guest rooms are offered in two recently renovated accommodation wings. Two modern self-contained double rooms, and four additional rooms without kitchen facilities are tastefully furnished with old fashioned comfort. A full cooked breakfast is served to all guests, even those with their own cooking facilities. The four additional rooms (two doubles and two singles) are located in the west wing and are complete with private facilities.

A guest lounge in the main house is a nice place to unwind after a busy day of skiing, fishing, bushwalking or taking in the sights of this historic area. A large orchard complements the array of roses, false acacias and other colorful blossoms in the formal garden area. There is even a courtyard fountain full of pretty goldfish.

Plans are currently underway to open a small deer park on the property, which will be available to guests only.

<table>
<tr><td>

CONTACT: Lorna & Allister Cowdery

PHONE: (003) 98 6213

BOOKING ADDRESS:
Strathmore Colonial Accommodation
Main Road
Nile, Tasmania 7212

PRICES: **$65 Double**
         $20 EAP

CREDIT CARDS: MC, VISA, AMEX, BC

BREAKFAST: Full cooked breakfast included

</td><td>

FACILITIES: All private

HANDICAPPED: Not recommended

PETS: Permitted with prior approval

OTHER: TV, heaters, some with full kitchen facilities, all with tea/coffee-making facilities, tennis court, off-street parking, phone on premises.

</td></tr>
</table>

AMELIA COTTAGE

(exclusively yours)
circa 1838
Oatlands, Midlands

Amelia Cottage, the oldest and largest cottage in the Waverley Collection, was built in 1838 by Thomas Burbury. Burbury was sent to Tasmania for crimes committed in England but was pardoned after risking his life to capture a sheep thief. He was granted land and built Amelia as his family home.

This colonial cottage is best described as authentically rustic. When you step over the weathered threshold, you will feel as if you have discovered a family cottage that was deserted and left untouched for a century. Only as you explore through the unusual artifacts will you come across modern conveniences, well hidden so as not to distract from the historic feeling of the place.

The cast-iron furnishings, original sandstone floors, a coal burning stove and vintage coach lanterns all contribute to the colonial feel of this marvellously restored cottage.

The upstairs sleeps eight comfortably and the ground floor has room for three. Perfect for a family or group holiday but intimate enough for just two.

CONTACT: Lyne Agnew

PHONE: (002) 54 1264

LOCATION:
104 High Street, Oatlands

BOOKING ADDRESS:
Amelia Cottage
Waverley Cottages
Oatlands, Tasmania 7120

PRICES: $65 Double
$15 EAP

CREDIT CARDS: VISA, BC

BREAKFAST: Ingredients for a cooked breakfast included

FACILITIES: Private

HANDICAPPED: No wheelchair access

PETS: Not permitted

OTHER: TV, heaters, full kitchen facilities, ample street parking, laundry available, no phone on premises.

FORGET-ME-NOT COTTAGE

(exclusively yours)
circa 1838/1986
Oatlands, Midlands

Incorporating three convict-built sandstone walls that were once the stables of the adjacent Amelia Cottage, Lyne Agnew created the Forget-Me-Not Cottage in 1986. Featuring floor-to-ceiling windows that give the cottage a sunny glow, the fourth wall and entry portico were constructed of recycled sandstone blocks. An old home near Tunbridge that was to be demolished supplied a wealth of recycled wood that has been artfully incorporated—baltic pine in the downstairs bedroom and bathroom, a huon pine sink and skirting boards, and bits and pieces of radiata pine and native Tasmanian woods give the cottage a special warmth.

The interior is an eclectic blend of old and new, designed round the forget-me-not theme. Tiny blue forget-me-not flowers cascade down the drapes and are accented by throw pillows in the same fabric. One wall is papered with a collection of old and antique greeting cards, all featuring forget-me-nots. Antique lovers will delight in many of the pieces on display, including an old phonograph, telephone, and a stereograph, complete with old photos. On a table next to the iron pot-bellied stove is a real treasure—a diary that once belonged to a departed Agnew ancestor, complete with dried flowers and poems.

Forget-Me-Not is an ideal escape for a romantic weekend for two, but can also accommodate four in its two bedrooms, one twin and one double.

CONTACT: Lyne Agnew

PHONE: (002) 54 1264

LOCATION:
17 Dulverstone Street, Oatlands

BOOKING ADDRESS:
Forget-Me-Not Cottage
Waverley Cottages
Oatlands, Tasmania 7120

PRICES: $65 Double
          $15 EAP

CREDIT CARDS: VISA, BC

BREAKFAST: Ingredients for a full
cooked breakfast included

FACILITIES: Private

HANDICAPPED: Not recommended
for wheelchairs

PETS: Not permitted

OTHER: TV, radio, full kitchen
facilities, heaters, off-street parking,
laundry available, no phone on
premises.

OATLANDS LODGE
circa 1837
Oatlands, Midlands

Legend has it that the woman who once owned a shop attached to what is now the Oatlands Lodge used plugs of tobacco to bribe the men constructing the main road through Oatlands to curve the road at that spot. She hoped the bend would slow traffic and attract customers to her shop.

This convict-built structure also housed a girls' school for a time, and most recently has been reincarnated as a comfortable guest lodge. Transplanted Californians Ray and Janet Lemos completely refurbished the decayed building, adding on a sunny breakfast room and installing the modern necessities. Today they offer travellers five rooms with private facilities (one single, one double, one twin and two family), a hearty home-cooked breakfast, and advice on where to hook the biggest trout. An avid 'fisho', Ray even hires out as a guide for fishing excursions.

All rooms have at least one wall displaying the original sandstone blocks of which the lodge is constructed; the convict stonemason's tool marks can still be seen in the blocks. Hand-made bricks in the entry hall bear the thumbprints of the unfortunate convicts who made them; close examination reveals the footprint of a colonial kitten in one brick!

Ray and Janet have also crafted many of the furnishings themselves; Ray constructed much of the colonial-style wood furniture and Janet made the quilts which decorate the beds. Guests can relax by the fire in the inviting sitting room after a day exploring the historic treasures found in Oatlands.

<table>
<tr><td>CONTACT: Ray & Janet Lemos</td><td>FACILITIES: All private</td></tr>
<tr><td>PHONE: (002) 54 1444</td><td>HANDICAPPED: Not recommended for wheelchairs</td></tr>
<tr><td>BOOKING ADDRESS:
Oatlands Lodge
92 High Street
Oatlands, Tasmania 7120</td><td>PETS: Not permitted</td></tr>
<tr><td>PRICES: $55 Double
           $45 Single
           $10 EAP</td><td>OTHER: TV in lounge, heaters, tea/ coffee available at all times, ample street parking, phone available.</td></tr>
<tr><td>CREDIT CARDS: MC, VISA, BC, AMEX</td><td></td></tr>
<tr><td>BREAKFAST: Full cooked breakfast included</td><td></td></tr>
</table>

WAVERLEY COTTAGE

(exclusively yours)
circa 1854
6 km outside Oatlands, Midlands

Situated on the Waverley farm amidst acres of rambling green countryside, Waverley Cottage is a special place that won't easily be forgotten. The cottage, together with the stables and the current Agnew home, were built in 1854 and used as workmen's cottages up until the 1930s. For the next thirty years, they underwent a period of deterioration and eventually became a windowless, doorless haven for animals and birds to escape the cold.

Looking at Waverley Cottage today it is difficult to imagine that this enchanting cottage was once in such a state of disrepair. Featured in *House and Garden* magazine in 1982, Waverley Cottage is a salvaged piece of history with the warmth and tranquillity of a bygone era. Lyne's love affair with her cottages began with Waverley, and her dedication is apparent as no detail is overlooked.

A double room and a colonial kitchen, complete with a stone bread oven, are on the ground floor. An attic room sleeps three and a comfy loft atop a steep staircase sleeps one. The cottage houses a unique collection of unusual artifacts, artfully crafted into furnishings by Lyne herself. A discarded copper vessel was polished and became a lampshade; a large huon pine desk once used by a grammar school was given new legs and now serves as the dining room table.

The old stables, which once housed Assyrian, a Melbourne Cup Winner, (who incidentally is buried by the gate of the Waverley farm) have been converted to a games room for the guests of Waverley Cottage and Waverley Croft.

There are plenty of games including table tennis and a pool table, but the real treasure is an old wooden doll's house with braille inscriptions.

CONTACT: Lyne Agnew

PHONE: (002) 54 1264

BOOKING ADDRESS:
Waverley Cottage
Oatlands, Tasmania 7120

PRICES: $65 Double
          $60 Single
          $15 EAP

CREDIT CARDS: VISA, BC

BREAKFAST: Ingredients for a full cooked breakfast included

FACILITIES: Private

HANDICAPPED: Wheelchair access with some assistance

PETS: Permitted with prior approval

OTHER: TV, radio, heaters, full kitchen facilities, laundry available, off-street parking, phone available at main house.

WAVERLEY CROFT
(exclusively yours)
circa 1982
6 km outside Oatlands, Midlands

The most personal of Lyne Agnew's Waverley Cottages, Waverley Croft was lovingly sculpted from local timber, recycled sandstone blocks that lay buried in a field for years, and hours of devotion to detail. All of the materials used to construct the cottage are recycled or are of local origin, except for the stained glass windows.

The handcrafted stained glass windows shine brilliantly in every room, giving the cottage the tranquillity of a tiny hillside chapel. Many of the furnishings are created from long forgotten pieces of the past. An ancient sewing machine base has been converted to a table. A wheel that was once part of this same machine hangs in the kitchen as a rack for various kitchen implements.

Cast-iron bedsteads dressed in handmade quilts and hand knitted blankets stand next to a marble top dressing table which displays old family photographs. The country pine kitchen even has an old telephone that you can crank up to call the main house on a party line.

Waverley Croft stands a stone's throw from Waverley Cottage, but is separated by a strand of trees that ensure privacy. Although it is a recent addition, Waverley Croft looks as if it has been part of the landscape for decades. This magical cottage sleeps three, but is the perfect escape for a romantic weekend for two!

<table>
<tr><td>

CONTACT: Lyne Agnew

PHONE: (002) 54 1264

BOOKING ADDRESS:
Waverley Cottages
Oatlands, Tasmania 7120

PRICES: $65 Double
          $60 Single
          $15 EAP

CREDIT CARDS: VISA, BC

BREAKFAST: Ingredients for a cooked breakfast included

</td><td>

FACILITIES: Private

HANDICAPPED: Designed to accommodate wheelchairs

PETS: Permitted with prior approval

OTHER: TV, radio, heaters, full kitchen facilities, laundry available, off-street parking, phone available at main house.

</td></tr>
</table>

HOLKHAM HOUSE

(exclusively yours)
circa 1870s
Orford, east coast

Built in the 1870s, Holkham House is one of the oldest houses on the picturesque east coast of Tasmania. Bordered by lemon trees on the outside and furnished in a comfortable country style, Holkham House is set amid ten acres on a peaceful hillside with enchanting views of the Prosser River. A perfect spot for a family gathering or a special holiday dinner, this beautiful home is spacious enough to accommodate fourteen people, but homey enough for just two.

There are two double rooms and one twin room on the ground floor and the upstairs attic is a wonderful escape for children who can keep themselves entertained for hours with an interesting collection of toys and games. The attic has two rooms and sleeps four.

Another unique feature is a games room, separate from the main house by just a few steps, complete with table tennis and other amusements. Ideal for older children who would love a night away from Mum and Dad, the games room also has two sets of bunk beds, sleeping four. A spacious kitchen, blessed with sunlight throughout the day, is stocked with ingredients for a hearty cooked breakfast.

A smaller hideaway, Miranda Cottage, was being created during our visit and should be available by the time of publication. More of an intimate retreat, Miranda has one double room and one twin room and is fully self-contained.

<table>
<tr><td>

CONTACT: Mrs. Anne Saunders

PHONE: (002) 25 1248

LOCATION:
Tasman Highway, Orford

BOOKING ADDRESS:
Holkham House
53 Waimea Avenue
Sandy Bay, Tasmania 7005

PRICES: $70 Double
** $12.50 EAP**
Reduced rate for children

CREDIT CARDS: None

BREAKFAST: Ingredients for a
cooked breakfast included

</td><td>

FACILITIES: Private (2 full
bathrooms)

HANDICAPPED: Wheelchair access
to Holkham House with minimal
assistance

PETS: Permitted with prior approval

OTHER: TV in lounge, heaters, full
kitchen facilities, parking, laundry
available, fireplace, tennis court, no
phone on premises.

</td></tr>
</table>

KERSBROOK HOST FARM

circa 1982
Pioneer, 110 km east of Launceston

Set in a tranquil clearing among towering trees, the main house at Kersbrook has a rustic colonial charm even though it was built in 1982. Surrounded by a wide verandah and a well-kept garden, Kersbrook is a perfect rural hideout from the cares of the city. Pioneer is located in the far north-east region of Tasmania, one hour from picturesque St. Helens on the east coast or half an hour from the north coast.

However, there is plenty to hold your interest on the farm. Owners Rita and Ian Summers always have a variety of interesting projects in various stages of completion. Restoration of antiques and vintage automobiles are favorite hobbies of Ian. The house holds quite a collection of restored radios and gramophones, including a 1924 Rexonola with prismaphonic speakers. Both are also avid book collectors and are quite musically inclined. The house is often the scene of musical gatherings in the evenings, and guests are always welcome to join in.

Accommodation is in the main house, in two comfortable guest rooms (one double, one single). Both are appointed with renovated turn-of-

the-century furniture and model sailing ships; one features a restored
1872 Packard pedal organ. A hearty farm style cooked breakfast is
included in the tariff, and is served family style in the warm kitchen.

CONTACT: Rita & Ian Summers

PHONE: (003) 54 2418

BOOKING ADDRESS:
Kersbrook Host Farm
Rita & Ian Summers
Gladstone Road
Pioneer, Tasmania 7264

PRICES: $48-60 Double
   (depending on the season)
         $25-32 Single
         $21 EAP
Reduced rate for children

CREDIT CARDS: None

BREAKFAST: Full cooked breakfast
included

FACILITIES: Shared

HANDICAPPED: Wheelchair access
with minimal assistance

PETS: Permitted with prior approval

OTHER: TV in lounge, heaters, tea/
coffee available at all times, laundry
available, off-street parking, phone on
premises.

CASCADES CONVICT OUT-STATION
(exclusively yours)
circa 1841
Koonya, Tasman Peninsula

In 1846 four hundred convicts and their overseers lived and toiled at the Cascades, 15 kilometres from the main settlement at Port Arthur. Established in 1841 as an agricultural and timber cutting out-station, the Cascades soon grew to include workshops, a hospital, chapel and rectory, stone quarries, quarters for married and unmarried soldiers, and of course cell blocks.

The remains of this settlement stand today on the 700 acre farm of Sue and Don Clark, who have painstakingly restored several of the buildings to provide one of the more unique types of accommodation in Australia. Guests are free to wander among the buildings and ruins, including a solitary confinement cell with the original iron bars in the windows. A private museum in one old workshop on the grounds contains a collection of Tasmanian apple crate labels and interesting artifacts and machinery found on the site during restoration, including a piece of a convict's shirt, and ancient iron tools. Guests can also take a bushwalk up to the site of the old timber mill, where convicts toiled in leg irons weighing up to forty pounds.

Accommodation is provided in five self-contained units; each includes ingredients for preparing your own continental breakfast. The Hospital is a large two-storey Georgian style home that can accommodate six people in three bedrooms. The best choice for a family, the Hospital is set in a lovely apple grove. Furnished in authentic colonial style, extras include a pool table, piano, trampoline and barbecue. (Two night minimum stay).

The three conjoined cottages of the Officers' Quarters won an Australian Heritage award in 1986. They each contain one bedroom and a combined kitchen and living room with a wood burning fireplace. The Overseer's Quarters nearby has a similar floor plan, with a double and single bed. Each has an authentic colonial decor and many lovely antiques. Brass and iron bedsteads are complemented by handmade quilts.

Be sure to read the fascinating historical information provided in each unit. The Clarks have managed to locate short biographies of soldiers and convicts stationed at the Cascades, as well as excerpts from the diary of a Quaker minister who visited the outstation in 1853. History, scenery, and pet sheep and chickens that beg for handouts—the Cascades is truly unique!

CONTACT: Sue & Don Clark

FACILITIES: Private

PHONE: (002) 50 3121

HANDICAPPED: Wheelchair access to Hospital accommodation with some assistance

BOOKING ADDRESS:
Cascades
RMB 1355, Koonya
Tasman Peninsula, Tasmania 7187

PETS: Not permitted

OTHER: TV, radio, heaters, full kitchen facilities, electric fans, off-street parking, fireplaces, minimum stay 2 nights in hospital unit.

PRICES: $60 Double
$50 Single
$15 EAP

CREDIT CARDS: None

BREAKFAST: Continental breakfast ingredients included

SEASCAPE
circa 1912
Arthur Highway (A9), 5 minutes from Port Arthur

Seascape is a pleasing combination of a beautiful home, a breathtaking location and the warm hospitality of hosts Sally and David Martin. The Martins spent two years renovating Seascape, a gracious white Federation style home with a pale pink roof and wide verandah framed in intricate iron lace trim. The grounds are a showcase—there are fruit trees of almost every variety and a small stream which trickles down a tiny waterfall through delicate flower gardens.

A delicious cooked breakfast, served in a sunny alcove of the kitchen overlooking an inlet of the Tasman Sea, includes a selection of homemade jams and usually a treat or two from the garden. The five rooms can accommodate up to ten guests in a friendly family atmosphere. The homey sitting room is warmed by a wood burning stove and is well stocked with interesting books on Tasmania's history and various attractions.

Both Sally and David are 'dinkie die' Tasmanians and take great pleasure in helping you plan your itinerary.

CONTACT: Sally & David Martin

PHONE: (002) 50 2367

BOOKING ADDRESS:
Seascape
Sally & David Martin
Port Arthur, Tasmania 7182

PRICES: $40 Double
          $25 Single
No children under 12

CREDIT CARDS: None

BREAKFAST: Full cooked breakfast
included

FACILITIES: Shared

HANDICAPPED: Wheelchair access
with some assistance

PETS: Not permitted

OTHER: TV in lounge, tea/coffee
available at all times, laundry
available by arrangement, off-street
parking, phone available.

TARANNA HOUSE
circa 1899
Taranna, Tasman Peninsula

Taranna House is a splendidly restored two-storey colonial farmhouse nestled on a gently sloping hillside overlooking an inlet of Norfolk Bay. Built in 1899 by the Quarrel family, the weatherboard house stands next to a small farm pond with a tiny landscaped island. Fragrant gardens surround the house; a small picnic table and a hammock are hidden there for restful afternoons.

The house is fully self-contained and the kitchen well stocked with spices and utensils. Taranna House is rented to one party at a time so there is no sharing of facilities. However, the owners (the Maxwell family of Evandale) keep a private apartment upstairs and occasionally spend a weekend there.

Taranna House is decorated with a turn-of-the-century grace and has many unique antique furnishings. A wooden rocking horse, an old doll's house, and a weathered seaman's chest are just a few of its treasures. A comfortable sitting room beckons in the evening with a pot belly stove and a wonderfully out-of-tune piano. The sitting room offers a postcard view of the bay; this same view can be enjoyed during fair weather from the compact front verandah.

Up to five people can be accommodated in three uniquely furnished bedrooms, one double, one single, and a twin. Taranna is located minutes from historic Port Arthur amid the scenic beauty of the Tasman Peninsula.

<table>
<tr><td>

CONTACT: Jane Maxwell

PHONE: (003) 91 8331 or
       (002) 50 3123

LOCATION:
Arthur Highway, Taranna

BOOKING ADDRESS:
Taranna House
Jane Maxwell
1 High Street
Evandale, Tasmania 7212

PRICES: $55 Double
         $27 Single
         $12 EAP

CREDIT CARDS: None

BREAKFAST: Ingredients for a
continental breakfast included

</td><td>

FACILITIES: Private

HANDICAPPED: Wheelchair access
with some assistance

PETS: Not permitted

OTHER: TV, heaters, full kitchen
facilities, laundry available, no phone
on premises. Reduced rate for longer
stays.

</td></tr>
</table>

LAUREL COTTAGE

(exclusively yours)
circa 1830
Richmond

Laurel Cottage takes its name from the arching laurel tree overhanging the front entrance. An idyllic colonial retreat on the edge of historic Richmond, the cottage stands a stone's throw from Australia's oldest bridge.

Fastidiously restored and furnished by Sandra and Wayne Barwick, Laurel Cottage is a special place. The sparkling bedrooms (one double, one twin) are dressed in white lace, accented by elegantly simple vanity sets on genuine colonial dressing tables. Victorian wedding photographs and a pair of linen bloomers hang on the wall in the master bedroom; the twin room displays a copy of Whistler's portrait of his mother. Several other sentimental heirlooms pay tribute to motherhood.

The creaking, uneven floor in the sitting room groans with each step; a bottle of port waits to be sampled while a fire blazes in the stone fireplace. In the morning, you can sip a cup of tea in the lovely garden amidst the flowering trees or enjoy a game of tennis on the private court if you feel energetic.

The kitchen contains a colonial pine dining set and kitchen dresser displaying a collection of china cups and unusual knick-knacks. Ingredients for a cooked breakfast are included in the tariff. An ideal base for exploring historic Richmond and the Midlands area, a stay at Laurel Cottage is an opportunity to relive a piece of history rather than just observe it.

CONTACT:Sandra & Wayne Barwick

PHONE: (002) 62 2454 or
    62 2357 (after hours)

BOOKING ADDRESS:
Laurel Cottage
Richmond, Tasmania 7025
15 Wellington Street

PRICES: $65 Double
           $15 EAP
           Reduced rate for children

CREDIT CARDS: None

BREAKFAST: Ingredients for a full cooked breakfast included

FACILITIES: Private

HANDICAPPED: Not recommended for wheelchairs

PETS: Not permitted

OTHER: Antique radio, heaters, full kitchen facilities, laundry available, parking, tennis court, no phone on premises

PROSPECT HOUSE
circa 1830s
Richmond

'A fine Game restaurant that also offers accommodation' is how owner/chef Graeme Phillips describes Prospect House. Graeme and wife Lil opened their award winning restaurant in 1980 in a hilltop Georgian mansion on the outskirts of Richmond.

Prospect House was built with convict labor in the mid 1830s for James Buscombe, owner of a nearby flour mill, pub, and grocery. The house had a succession of owners, including an eccentric English colonel fresh from colonial India. He fired cannons on the front lawn to welcome V.I.P.s. Several cannonballs were unearthed during the renovation of the house and grounds.

Described by some as the finest restaurant in the state, Prospect House's wine cellar (converted from the old convicts' quarters) boasts arguably the finest selection of Tasmanian wines in Australia. The menu changes with the seasons, but specializes in game in interesting combinations of flavor and texture. The current menu features Tasmanian venison with juniper berries, parsnip chips and celeriac puree; other selections include wild duck, guinea fowl, and ocean trout ravioli.

Accommodation is offered in seven double and three twin rooms overlooking a sunny courtyard, ideal for relaxation and enjoyment of a good book. Guest units were constructed in 1981 from what were once the barn and haylofts; all are simply furnished with colonial syle decor, and have private facilities.

Guests can enjoy their continental breakfast featuring a selection of freshly baked pastries in one of two dining rooms in the main house, in their own room, or in the courtyard.

CONTACT: Graeme & Lil
  Phillips

PHONE: (002) 62 2207

BOOKING ADDRESS:
Prospect House
Richmond, Tasmania 7025

PRICES: Double: $175 Dinner, Bed & Breakfast
$80 Bed & Breakfast
$65 Room Only
Single: $62.50 Bed & Breakfast
$55 Room Only
(Dinner includes an unlimited choice from the menu, excluding wine and spirits)
Reduced rate for children

CREDIT CARDS: VISA, MC, BC

FACILITIES: All private

HANDICAPPED: Wheelchair access to five ground floor rooms, one fully equipped to accommodate wheelchairs

PETS: Not permitted

OTHER: TV, heaters, minibars, refrigerators, tea/coffee-making facilities, laundry available, ample off-street parking, tennis court. Fully licensed restaurant open for dinner seven nights a week and for lunch on Sundays; closed in July

THE DISPENSARY

(exclusively yours)
circa 1830
Richmond

The Dispensary was originally built in the 1830s to service the neighboring old Richmond Gaol. Dr. John Coverdale was appointed assistant surgeon in 1840 and began planting an extensive herb garden at the back of the tiny cottage to supply many of the medicines he used. The front porch of The Dispensary served as a waiting room for his patients; the good Doctor was also responsible for the prisoners in the gaol. Today, the cottage is situated in a quiet section of Richmond, away from the crowds that throng the main street. Nearby are St. Luke's Church, the Old Rectory, numerous historic houses and, of course, the Old Gaol (now a museum).

The two-room cottage (a kitchen, one bedroom that sleeps four, and a bathroom) has been restored and furnished with a colonial ambience and all the modern conveniences. The fully equipped kitchen is stocked with everything for a hearty country breakfast, including fresh eggs and homemade jams.

An ideal hideaway for two, The Dispensary is a good starting place for many lovely walks; two private tennis courts are also available.

The Dispensary even comes equipped with a friendly dog who will join you on the back porch overlooking the Coal River and surrounding countryside.

<table>
<tr><td>

CONTACT: Starr Oclee

PHONE: (002) 62 2226

BOOKING ADDRESS:
The Old Rectory
Edward Street
Richmond, Tasmania 7025

PRICES: $70 Double
** $10 EAP**

CREDIT CARDS: None

BREAKFAST: Ingredients for a full
cooked breakfast included

</td><td>

FACILITIES: Private

HANDICAPPED: Wheelchair access
with minimal assistance

PETS: Permitted with prior approval,
kennel behind cottage

OTHER: TV, radio, heaters, full
kitchen facilities, laundry available at
Old Rectory next door, parking, no
phone on premises

</td></tr>
</table>

TAMAR HOUSE
circa 1978
Rosevears, 20 minutes north of Launceston

High on a hill overlooking the beautiful Tamar River and surrounded by two and a half acres of lush gardens, Tamar House is a rambling country estate. A garden lover's nirvana, the formal gardens are criss-crossed by brick pathways among the roses, young magnolia trees, and trellised wisteria. A cornucopia of fruits, nuts, and vegetables appears in season, including passion fruit, strawberries, apples, nectarines, gooseberries, almonds, walnuts, kiwi, various citrus fruit and others too numerous to mention.

Another feature sure to delight those with a green thumb is the spacious fernery, a brick floored, glass walled room with exposed ceiling timbers that support an extensive collection of ferns and other delicate plants. This relaxing retreat serves as a sitting room for guests, complete with a TV, organ, and lounge chairs.

Accommodation is in two rooms in a separate wing of the tile roofed brick house. Hosts Mary and Ray Oxford plan to add two additional rooms in 1988. Be sure to ask for the room with a view of the gardens and river. Breakfast is served in the dining room of the main house, which takes full advantage of the postcard views from the property. Dinner is also available by arrangement.

Tamar House is twenty minutes from Launceston and is close to the Grindelwald Swiss Village, local vineyards and a bird sanctuary.

<table>
<tr><td>

CONTACT: Mary & Ray Oxford

PHONE: (003) 30 1744

BOOKING ADDRESS:
Tamar House
Rosevears Drive
Rosevears, Tasmania 7277

PRICES: **$50 Double**
          $40 Single
          $15 EAP
Reduced rate for children, discount for longer stays

CREDIT CARDS: MC, BC

BREAKFAST: Full cooked breakfast included

</td><td>

FACILITIES: Private

HANDICAPPED: Wheelchair access with some assistance

PETS: Not permitted

OTHER: TV, radios, heaters, tea/coffee-making facilities, laundry available, off-street parking, phone at main house

</td></tr>
</table>

HAWTHORN COTTAGE ROSS

(exclusively yours)
circa 1910
Ross, Midlands

The classic Federal style exterior of this cosy cottage hides an interior that is decorated in a posh, modern style. Built in 1910 by the Tacey family, Hawthorn Cottage stands in the heart of Ross. The cottage is an excellent base for exploring the historic Midlands area; guests can begin by exploring the sights of Ross on bicycles found in the shed behind the house. Century-old churches, the famous convict-built Ross bridge, and several tea rooms and craft shops are just down the street.

The cottage is a perfect hideaway for two, but can accommodate a family of six in two bedrooms (a double and a quad with four bunk beds). A comfy living room furnished in a muted pink features a stone fireplace and a sunny bay window overlooking the main street of Ross.

A second fireplace warms the spacious kitchen and adjacent dining area, both finished in handsome pine. A few unusual antiques and other knick-knacks are displayed on the mantel.

Breakfast is not included, but owner Maryann Keach has been known to drop by on occasion with fresh eggs and milk.

<table>
<tr><td>

CONTACT: Maryann Keach

PHONE: (003) 81 5225

BOOKING ADDRESS:
Hawthorn Cottage Ross
Church Street
Ross, Tasmania 7209

PRICES: $50 Double
** $35 Single**
** $10 EAP**

CREDIT CARDS: None

BREAKFAST: Not included

</td><td>

FACILITIES: Private

HANDICAPPED: Wheelchair access
with minimal assistance

PETS: Not permitted

OTHER: TV, heaters, full kitchen
facilities, parking, laundry available,
bicycles available for guests' use, no
phone on premises

</td></tr>
</table>

HUDSON COTTAGE

(exclusively yours)
circa 1850
Ross, Midlands

This showpiece colonial cottage was condemned and about to be demolished when it was rescued by local antique dealer and historian Tim Johnson and his wife, Sue. The ramshackle two bedroom shearers' cottage housed nine people and eight dogs as recently as 1980, but had dirt floors and no electricity or plumbing. Cooking and heating of water for bathing was done over an open fire!

After installing electricity and modern kitchen and bathroom facilities, the Johnsons lived in the cottage while completing the massive renovation job. The rustic sandstone blocks were covered in layers of paint; the only way to remove it was to painstakingly chip it away with the blunt side of an axe.

The interior today is a marvellous collection of antiques and memorabilia; Tim encourages guests to touch and 'play with' anything that catches their fancy. Guests can crank up a tune on a vintage gramophone, play a 1940s era Monopoly game, or read the 1916 newspapers that line an old wooden trunk. If that sounds too strenuous, you may want to look at old-time photos through a stereo viewer while lounging in a Tasmanian blackwood rocking chair next to a pot-belly stove named 'Fatso'.

Splendid colonial cedar furniture, unique century-old bottles, and other one-of-a-kind treasures beckon from all directions. Bedrooms (one double, one twin) are furnished with graceful iron beds and handmade quilts; floors are covered in oval rugs hand-woven from old clothing.

And if all that weren't enough, Tim happens to be the local historian and gives excellent guided walking tours of Ross to various tour groups. A wonderful storyteller and knowledgeable guide, he offers guests staying a week or more a free walking tour. One couple was so enchanted with Hudson Cottage, they cancelled all other bookings for the next week to stay there!

Tim and Sue are currently restoring a second cottage in Ross and plan to open it for business by the end of 1988. Thirteen babies were born to the same overworked mother in the front room of that 1880 weatherboard cottage; five still live in the Ross area. Tim promises the Apple Dumpling Cottage will be just as irresistable as Hudson Cottage—plan to book early!

CONTACT: Tim & Sue Johnson

PHONE: (003) 81 5354

BOOKING ADDRESS:
Hudson Cottage
Main Street
Ross, Tasmania 7209

PRICES: $64 Double
** $10 EAP**

CREDIT CARDS: None

BREAKFAST: Ingredients for a cooked breakfast included

FACILITIES: Private

HANDICAPPED: Wheelchair access with minimal assistance

PETS: Outside only, with prior approval

OTHER: TV available on request (don't you dare!), radio, heaters, full kitchen facilities, laundry, off-street parking, small back yard. Phone located across the street.

GATEFORTH COTTAGE

(exclusively yours)
property circa 1840, cottage modern
Black River, near Stanley, north-west coast

Gateforth Farm was established in 1840, the first land settled in the area by Europeans outside the Van Diemen's Land Company holdings. The property has remained in the Medwin family since that first settlement; Rodney and Christine Medwin are the fifth generation of the family to work this land. They still live in the 1870s era main homestead and graze sheep and beef cattle and raise various crops on the property.

Gateforth Cottage is a modern self-contained brick structure nestled on top of a neighboring hillside with a million dollar view of the coast all the way to the famous 'Nut' at Stanley. An ideal spot for families with children or for travellers seeking privacy and seclusion, Gateforth offers a myriad activities for those so inclined.

Guests can catch a trout in the pond down the hill, bushwalk, gather oysters in the nearby estuary or observe various farming activities. Christine is well known for her culinary skills; guests can order picnic baskets containing homemade prawn quiche, fresh fruit salads, and

Tasmanian cider. A fully equipped kitchen and barbecue are available; barbecue packs and breakfast packs can also be arranged for an extra charge.

The cottage contains three bedrooms, two with twin beds and one with a double. Up to six more people can be accommodated in an adjacent bungalow. The main cottage features a pot-belly stove, fresh flowers, and a selection of toys and family games. To complete this home away from home there is even a cat that has adopted the cottage and will come around at mealtime.

CONTACT: Christine & Rodney Medwin

PHONE: (004) 58 3230

BOOKING ADDRESS:
Gateforth
Christine & Rodney Medwin
Black River, Tasmania 7321

PRICES: $50 Double
$40 Single
$10 EAP
Reduced rate for children

CREDIT CARDS: None

BREAKFAST: Not included, available by arrangement

FACILITIES: Private, bathroom with separate toilet

HANDICAPPED: Wheelchair access with minimum assistance

PETS: Not permitted

OTHER: TV, radio, heaters, full kitchen facilities, ample parking, trout fishing, farm activities, picnic baskets, BBQ, phone available at main house.

HARBOUR MASTER'S COTTAGE

(exclusively yours)
circa 1880
Stanley, north-west coast

Nestled just above the serenity of Tatlow's Beach, the Harbour Master's Cottage was originally the home of Mr. Edwards, Stanley's early harbour master. The one-storey cottage is surrounded by a picket fence which leads to the rear of the home, where you will discover a delightful private garden. A perfect place for a quiet afternoon picnic, the garden ends where the 'Nut', a towering volcanic formation and landmark of the north-west coast, begins.

The Harbour Master's Cottage, with its pine floors held together by handmade nails, is an authentically restored piece of history. Lovingly returned to its original colonial state, it is tastefully furnished with period antiques and, of course, fresh cut flowers.

The rooms, one double and two twin, are exquisitely simple and all have wood burning fireplaces with ample firewood at your disposal. After waking up in the morning to a lovely view of the sea and surrounding lush hillsides, you can make your way to the homey kitchen/ sitting room where fresh ingredients are supplied for a hearty cooked breakfast.

CONTACT: Mrs. Maureen Kennedy **FACILITIES:** Private

PHONE: (004) 58 1301 or 52 1769

BOOKING ADDRESS:
Harbour Master's Cottage
42 Alexander Terrace
Stanley, Tasmania 7331

PRICES: $55 Double
$5 EAP

CREDIT CARDS: MC, VISA, BC

BREAKFAST: Ingredients for a full
cooked breakfast included

HANDICAPPED: Wheelchair access
with some assistance

PETS: Not permitted

OTHER: TV in sitting room, heaters,
full kitchen facilities, laundry
available, parking, no phone on
premises

LAUGHTON HOUSE
circa 1906
Stanley, north-west coast

Laughton House was built in 1906 by Stanley's first solicitor, Kenric Laughton. Overlooking Godfrey's Beach and the Nut, Laughton House was inhabited by descendants of Kenric Laughton until 1984.

Maureen Kennedy (also owner of the neighboring Harbour Master's Cottage) has done an exquisite job of restoring this gracious Edwardian house to its former glory. Much of the handsome cedar furniture in the guest rooms and the picture perfect dining room were originally in the house.

During the restoration many precious heirlooms were discovered in an underground storeroom, including fragile porcelain dolls, a child's rocking chair, and old family photographs now on display in the dining room. Several elegant dresses and turn-of-the-century costumes are also on display in the spacious hallway.

The six guest rooms are exceptionally bright and airy and fresh flowers add a special touch. Request the double room at the front of the house to enjoy a brilliant sunrise peeking through the lace curtains of your bay window while relaxing in a graceful cast-iron bed. All rooms feature private facilities, antique furnishings, and tea/coffee-making facilities.

Delicious cooked breakfasts are served in the elegant dining room; guests can also sip a cup of tea on the lovely wide verandah.

CONTACT: Mrs. Maureen Kennedy

PHONE: (004) 58 1301 or 52 1769

BOOKING ADDRESS:
Laughton House
45 Church Street
Stanley, Tasmania 7331

PRICES: $60 Double
          $50 Single
          $10 EAP
Reduced rate for children

CREDIT CARDS: MC, VISA, BC

BREAKFAST: Full cooked breakfast included

FACILITIES: All private

HANDICAPPED: Wheelchair access with some assistance

PETS: Not permitted

OTHER: TV, heaters, tea/coffee-making facilities, laundry available, ample street parking, phone on premises

MONATERIC
circa 1890
1 km west of Wiltshire, north-west coast

The Monateric combines colonial appeal with spectacular scenery and a working farm where you can milk a cow or assist in birthing a lamb. Monateric was the aboriginal name for the Nut at nearby Stanley, the dominant geological formation of the north-west coast. The location of the house offers a postcard view of the Nut across an inlet of the sea, where guests may gather clams or oysters for an evening meal. (Dinner by arrangement.)

The property where Monateric is located was originally settled in 1843 by H. J. Emmett, a storekeeper for the Van Diemen's Land Company and later secretary to Governor Franklin. At least six families have called the property home since then.

The house would provide a marvellous setting for an Agatha Christie novel. Furnishings are simple and country comfortable. One room boasts original cedar cabinets, a handmade blackwood and walnut bed, and a seaman's chest belonging to host Barkley Walker's grandfather.

Fresher eggs and milk for breakfast could not be found; homemade jams come from whatever is ripe in the garden. The mildness of the north-west coast's climate allows fruits ranging from kiwis to cumquats to grow here; the freshly squeezed orange juice you enjoy at breakfast may have come from a tree in the garden that morning.

The gracious hosts of Monateric, Norma and Barkley Walker, are happy to complete the history of the property and supply you with gumboots for a walk round the farm and through the lovely gardens. Plan to stay more than one night—you'll regret leaving too soon.

CONTACT: Norma & Barkley Walker

PHONE: (004) 58 3248

BOOKING ADDRESS:
Monateric
P.O. Box 33
Stanley, Tasmania 7331

PRICES: $50 Double
$30 Single
$20 EAP
Reduced rate for children

CREDIT CARDS: None

BREAKFAST: Full cooked breakfast included

FACILITIES: Private

HANDICAPPED: Wheelchair access with some assistance

PETS: Not permitted

OTHER: TV in sitting room, radio, heaters, tea/coffee available at all times, laundry available, ample parking, phone available

TOUCHWOOD COTTAGE
circa 1836
Stanley, north-west coast

Built at the foot of Stanley's famous Nut in 1836 by five brothers, Touchwood is one of historic Stanley's oldest homes. This comfortable cottage is furnished with period antiques and bits and pieces of history collected by its owners, Maisie and Greg, who live on the premises.

Touchwood Cottage has been lovingly restored to its original state which mysteriously includes an odd-shaped sitting room and doorways with varying heights. There are two double rooms and one twin room, each with its own unique charm.

A cooked breakfast complete with freshly squeezed orange juice and homemade cereals is served in the kitchen, where guests are made to feel a part of the family.

Maisie and Greg also keep themselves busy with Touchwood Craft Shop next door, said by authorities to be one of the best in Australia. And if that weren't enough, Maisie is also an accomplished folk singer and has recently organized a local folk singer's club.

CONTACT: Maisie Ferguson
and Greg Taylor

PHONE: (004) 58 1348

BOOKING ADDRESS:
Touchwood Cottage
33 Church Street
Stanley, Tasmania 7331

PRICES: $50 Double
            $30 Single
            $15 EAP

CREDIT CARDS: MC, VISA, BC

BREAKFAST: Full cooked breakfast
included

FACILITIES: Shared

HANDICAPPED: No wheelchair
access

PETS: Not permitted

OTHER: TV/Radio in sitting room,
heaters, tea/coffee available at all
times, laundry available, dinner by
arrangement, ample street parking,
phone on premises, discount at
Touchwood Craft Shop

FRANKLIN MANOR

circa 1888
Strahan, west coast

Although its extensive renovations and structural modifications were still in process at the time we stumbled across Franklin Manor, if all goes according to plan it will soon become one of Tasmania's premier retreats.

Scheduled to open in late 1988, this posh two-storey manor was a classic weatherboard house that once belonged to the local harbour master. Modernized inside and expanded to accommodate the fussiest travellers, the ten double rooms will all be equipped with telephones, fireplaces, minibars, cassette players, and televisions complete with in-house movies. Some rooms will have private spas and there is even a suite designed for the executive who just can't leave home without his personal computer.

The ground floor is the site of the formal, fully licensed restaurant and cocktail lounge. The menu of chef Laine Willis will emphasize excellent local Tasmanian produce, game, and seafoods served on china and lace with all the trimmings. The basement is being converted to an expansive wine cellar, where guests can sample different vintages before choosing one to accompany their evening meal.

Franklin Manor is set in three acres of gardens planted in native trees and shrubs, with winding footpaths and shady benches hidden among the ferns. The grounds also sport generous fruit trees and a pond where a platypus has already taken up residence. Historical purists may raise an eyebrow at how this 1890s home has been modernised; others will find it to be just the luxurious retreat with a difference that they have been searching for.

<table>
<tr><td>

CONTACT: Laine Willis

PHONE: (004) 71 7247

FAX: (004) 71 7267

BOOKING ADDRESS:
Franklin Manor
The Esplanade
Strahan, Tasmania 7468

PRICES: Begin at $90 per person, Bed and Breakfast
Rooms with spas add an additional $30
No children under thirteen

CREDIT CARDS: MC, VISA, BC

BREAKFAST: Full cooked breakfast included

</td><td>

FACILITIES: All private

HANDICAPPED: Two rooms fully equipped to accommodate wheelchairs

PETS: Not permitted

OTHER: TV, radio, tea/coffee-making facilities in all rooms, fireplaces, minibars, in-house movies, spas in some rooms, gourmet licensed restaurant, cocktail bar, telephones, refrigerators, parking.

</td></tr>
</table>

LESTER COTTAGES

(exclusively yours)
circa 1880
Swansea, east coast

The Lester Cottage complex began with the restoration of the 1880s era colonial house now known as Lester Cottage. This Georgian style stone cottage was built by the Rapp brothers, part of a large group of German immigrants who arrived in the Swansea area at that time. Restored by Peter and Helen Morey, Lester Cottage is now the cornerstone of a complex of six cottages, a home, and a barn overlooking Oyster Bay and the rugged peaks of Freycinet National Park.

Two-storey Lester Cottage is attached to the Morey's home, and a cooked breakfast is served in the dining room. Furnished in colonial style with many antiques, the cottage has no kitchen but does feature private facilities and a cosy sitting room with a fireplace.

Five modern self-contained cottages with a colonial feel have been constructed on the site, each with its own unique features. Pine Cottage has been specifically designed to accommodate disabled guests and features a full kitchen, breakfast ingredients, and double and single beds in its ground floor bedroom.

The intimate Hayloft is perched above Pine Cottage. The two are often rented by couples travelling together, or the Hayloft can be a cosy hideaway for two, with private facilities and ingredients for a continental breakfast due to limited kitchen facilities.

Cedar Cottage is a family unit, with two bedrooms and a spacious sitting room. The upstairs bedroom contains a lacy iron and brass double bed with a matching crib; the downstairs bedroom holds double and single beds. A full kitchen is stocked with ingredients for a cooked breakfast.

The two Oak Cottages are built on the site of what was once the blacksmith's shop, and were specifically designed for couples. Both have a charming colonial feeling; one with a double bed, the other with two singles and both with facilities for preparation of light meals.

The entire complex is surrounded by a colonial stone fence and the beautiful grounds are lush with flowers and ornamental shrubs.

CONTACT: Peter & Helen Morey

PHONE: (002) 57 8105

BOOKING ADDRESS:
Lester Cottages
50 Gordon Street
Swansea, Tasmania 7190

PRICES: $65 Double
** $20 EAP**
Reduced rate for children

CREDIT CARDS: MC, VISA, BC

BREAKFAST: Cooked breakfast
**   (Lester Cottage)**
**   Breakfast ingredients**
**   (Others)**

FACILITIES: Private

HANDICAPPED: Wheelchair access
to Pine Cottage only

PETS: Not permitted

OTHER: TV, radio, heaters, tea/
coffee-making facilities (some with full
kitchen facilities), refrigerator,
laundry available, off-street parking,
phone available at main house.
Minimum booking of four days during
Christmas and Easter holidays.

MEREDITH HOUSE
circa 1853
Swansea, east coast

After more than 10,000 hours of gruelling labor, the present owners of Meredith House have restored a showpiece to its original grandeur. Originally known as Laughton House in the 1850s, the home was first occupied by a local surveyor and was eventually sold for use as a Girls' Grammar School. Several additions have taken place throughout the years, as it was also a Baby Hospital, a private residence and, finally, a guest house. Over the years, deterioration of the building made it almost un-salvageable and the National Trust termed it something of a disaster.

Fortunately in 1987, Canberra, as it was then called, was purchased by the present owners who spent eight long months replacing, connecting, building, cleaning and polishing every inch of this home until it was restored to a 'colonial classic.' Striking hand crafted red cedar furniture and the warm comfortable atmosphere all add to a memorable experience at Meredith House.

A pleasant change from the usual eggs and bacon breakfast, Meredith House offers an unusual breakfast menu which changes with the seasons. In the evening, the lovely breakfast room turns into an intimate restaurant serving a delicious three-course meal including a complimentary bottle of wine.

Meredith House has four double rooms, some complete with wash basin and refrigerator, and two twin rooms.

CONTACT: Bill & Helen Tinning and Craig & Joanne Brown

PHONE: (002) 57 8119

BOOKING ADDRESS:
Meredith House
15 Noyes Street
Swansea, Tasmania 7190

PRICES: $50 Double
$40 Single
$10 EAP
Reduced rate for children

CREDIT CARDS: MC, VISA, BC

BREAKFAST: Full cooked breakfast included

FACILITIES: Shared

HANDICAPPED: No wheelchair access

PETS: Not permitted

OTHER: TV in lounge, tea/coffee-making facilities, some rooms with refrigerators, laundry available, off-street parking, BYO restaurant, phone on premises

OYSTER BAY GUEST HOUSE
circa 1836
Swansea, east coast

Overlooking beautiful Oyster Bay and Freycinet National Park, this charming colonial guest house offers unique old-world accommodation and warm hospitality. The structure was built in 1836 and was originally known as the Black Swan Inn. Today the Oyster Bay Guest House offers travellers a genteel resting place and a first class licensed restaurant on site.

Stained glass windows, rich woodwork and fresh flowers complement handsome antique furniture in the common areas. The ten guest rooms are tastefully decorated in white lace, with a sprinkling of antiques, turn-of-the-century books and more fresh flowers. Various combinations of single, double, and family rooms are available, some with private facilities.

The Shy Albatross Restaurant on the ground floor specializes in innovative cuisine that makes the most of the freshest Tasmanian produce and seafoods, prepared with French and Italian influences. Delicious hot bread and an extensive wine list complement the well chosen entrees and main courses that change with the seasons. Friendly service and lush house plants give the restaurant an intimate appeal.

After dinner, you can relax in the lounge by a fire in winter or retire to the upstairs verandah with a hot cup of tea.

CONTACT: Suzanne & Michael Williamson

PHONE: (002) 57 8110

BOOKING ADDRESS:

Oyster Bay Guest House
10 Franklin Street
Swansea, Tasmania 7190

PRICES: **$40-60 Double**
$30 Single
$10 EAP

CREDIT CARDS: VISA, MC, BC, DC

BREAKFAST: Full cooked breakfast included

FACILITIES: Some rooms with private facilities, others share

HANDICAPPED: No wheelchair access

PETS: Permitted outside only, with prior approval

OTHER: TV in lounge, heaters, off-street parking, licensed restaurant on premises (Open Monday-Saturday in summer, Tuesday-Saturday in winter, bookings required), phone available nearby. Closed December 25, 26.

ROSE COTTAGE and
STONEMASON'S COTTAGE

(each exclusively yours)
circa 1860
Lisdillon Estate, 20 km south of Swansea

Although both the Rose and the Stonemason's Cottages were built in 1860 and have similar characteristics each has its own unique charm and distinctions.

Perfect for a family holiday, Rose Cottage is the larger of the two. The cottage was originally built as the post office for the historic Lisdillon Estate, and the small window in the sitting room once served as the postal counter. A short history of the estate is framed on the nearby wall for interested guests. There are two attic bedrooms with sloped ceilings and small windows with refreshing views of the surrounding landscape and gardens. The walls are decorated with old black and white photographs of early settlers. The original post office, now the sitting room, has a selection of old books and magazines that you can enjoy while spending a quiet evening by the fire.

For those with a little romance in mind, the Stonemason's Cottage is an intimate hideaway for two, overlooking the sea on a semi-private beach. The cottage was originally built for the resident stonemason in 1860, and has been carefully restored to preserve the atmosphere of the colonial era. Antique furnishings, open fires and the quiet peace of the Tasmanian countryside are just a part of the charm of this tiny cottage. Although it stands next to the home of the Sinclair family, you'll feel as if you're all alone at the Stonemason's Cottage.

CONTACT: Dianne Sinclair

PHONE: (002) 57 7576 or 57 8331

BOOKING ADDRESS:
Rose Cottage or Stonemason's
  Cottage
Dianne Sinclair
Lisdillon via Triabunna
Tasmania 7273

PRICES: **$65 Double**
          $60 Single
          $10 EAP

CREDIT CARDS: None

BREAKFAST: Ingredients for a
cooked breakfast supplied on request

FACILITIES: Private

HANDICAPPED: Wheelchair access
to Rose Cottage with assistance
No wheelchair access to Stonemason's
Cottage, bedroom is upstairs

PETS: Permitted with prior approval

OTHER: TV in lounge, radio, heaters,
full kitchen facilities, laundry
available, off-street parking, no phone
on premises, minimum stay of 4 days
over Easter holidays, 3 days over long
weekends

WAGNER'S COTTAGES

(exclusively yours)
circa 1860 and 1986
outskirts of Swansea

The two Wagner's Cottages are set in beautiful Tasmanian countryside overlooking Oyster Bay. The Stone Cottage was built in 1860 by German immigrant Michael Wagner. A charming two-storey structure with what may very well be the steepest staircase in Australia, this original cottage has been carefully restored to retain an old world atmosphere. Across the well-tended garden stands the Brick Cottage, a modern hideaway constructed in the old style with a feeling of yesterday.

The ground floor of the Stone Cottage has a twin bedroom, a fully equipped kitchen, and a quaint sitting room complete with a crackling open fire. Up the ladder-like staircase is found another bedroom with double and single beds. The entire cottage is filled with antiques and memorabilia, such as a working pot-belly stove and an ancient sewing machine.

A few steps away is Wagner's Brick Cottage, lovingly created in 1986 by owner Dianne Sinclair. Dianne also owns the Rose and Stonemason's Cottages, twenty kilometers away at the Lisdillon Estate.

Wagner's Brick Cottage sleeps four in one double room and one twin room. Similar in decor and ambience to the Stone Cottage, this cottage captures the charm of colonial days and is also fully self-contained.

Both cottages include ingredients for a full cooked breakfast on request. The cottages are available year round, but require a minimum booking of four days at Easter; long holiday weekends must be booked for the entire weekend.

CONTACT: Dianne Sinclair

PHONE: (002) 57 7576 or 57 8331

BOOKING ADDRESS:
Wagner's Cottages
Dianne Sinclair
Lisdillon, via Triabunna
Tasmania 7273

PRICES: $65 Double
** $60 Single**
** $10 EAP**
Reduced rate for children

CREDIT CARDS: None

BREAKFAST: Ingredients for a
cooked breakfast supplied on request

FACILITIES: Private

HANDICAPPED: Wheelchair access to both cottages with minimal assistance

PETS: Permitted with prior approval

OTHER: TV, radio, heaters, full kitchen facilities, laundry available, off-street parking, minimum stay of 4 nights during Easter holidays, 3 nights over long weekends, nearest phone is in Swansea, 5 minutes from the cottages.

OCEAN VIEW GUEST HOUSE

circa 1903
Ulverstone, north coast

Located two blocks from a pleasant beach facing Bass Strait, the Ocean View is a good choice for a seaside holiday. You can actually see the ocean from some of the nine guest rooms (two single, four double, one family room with a double and single bed, and two twin rooms).

Built in 1903, this stately house served as a boarding house for most of its life. Converted into a guest house in 1986, the whole house was 'done over' following a change of ownership in February of 1988. Crisp new paint and wallpaper complements carefully selected antique furnishings with some modern reproductions to maintain the turn-of-the-century feeling.

Some rooms feature wood burning fireplaces; a cosy sitting room downstairs also offers a fire in winter. A full cooked breakfast is served in a cheery dining room. At night, the dining room becomes Angela's BYO Restaurant. The blackboard menu features a choice of varying main courses, two soups, vegies, and five or six desserts. Three-course meals are a fixed $15, four courses are $17. Afternoon teas can be arranged for groups as well.

At this time, all facilities are communal; owners Jeff and Jenny Foster plan to convert all to en suite in 1989.

<table>
<tr><td>

CONTACT: Jeff & Jenny Foster

PHONE: (004) 25 5401

BOOKING ADDRESS:
Ocean View Guest House
1-3 Victoria Street
Ulverstone, Tasmania 7315

PRICES: **$37 Double**
           $27 Single
           $10 EAP
Reduced rate for children

CREDIT CARDS: MC, VISA, BC, AMEX, DC

BREAKFAST: Full cooked breakfast included

</td><td>

FACILITIES: Shared

HANDICAPPED: Wheelchair access with minimal assistance

PETS: Not permitted

OTHER: TV in lounge, heaters, tea/coffee available at all times, laundry available, BYO restaurant on premises, ample parking, working fireplaces in some rooms, phone on premises

</td></tr>
</table>

EGMONT

(exclusively yours)
circa 1838
Westbury, 20 minutes west of Launceston

A stay at Egmont is like a visit to a great-grandmother's farm cottage. Perched on a quiet, sunny hillside beneath the overhanging branches of a century-old oak tree, this historic home is unique in that it has remained in the same family for five generations. The Greenhill family have preserved a piece of history by maintaining original furnishings throughout, including one-of-a-kind heirlooms and old family photographs.

The comfortable sitting room and two of the four bedrooms have wood-burning fireplaces that have been in use since the 1800s. The original eucalypt wood floors and narrow staircase have worn smooth through decades of use. There is even a stone windowsill in the kitchen with grooves worn into it from a century of use as a knife sharpener. The two ground floor bedrooms and two attic bedrooms are simply decorated with antique beds and many interesting artifacts.

Stepping outside to the front verandah, you can hear the Meander River below and enjoy a beautiful view of rolling countryside, ruins of the old Egmont flour mill and roaming livestock. You can go for

a bushwalk, fish or swim in the nearby river, or simply enjoy the peace
and tranquillity of your very own cottage.

CONTACT: Virginia Greenhill

PHONE: (003) 93 1164 or 93 1622

BOOKING ADDRESS:
Egmont
Birralee Road 922
Westbury, Tasmania 7303

PRICES: $45 Double
** $10 EAP**
Reduced rate for children

CREDIT CARDS: None

BREAKFAST: Not included

FACILITIES: Private

HANDICAPPED: No wheelchair
access

PETS: Not permitted

OTHER: TV in sitting room, heaters,
full kitchen facilities, laundry
available, off-street parking, no phone
on premises.

ALPHABETICAL LISTING OF ACCOMMODATION (INDEX)

Name:	City:
AIRLIE HOUSE	Launceston
ALICE'S PLACE	Launceston
AMELIA COTTAGE	Oatlands
BARTON COTTAGE	Battery Point (Hobart)
BENTLEY COTTAGE	Chudleigh
BOATWRIGHT HOUSE	Launceston
BONNEY'S INN	Deloraine
BRICKENDON COTTAGE	Longford
CASCADES CONVICT OUT-STATION	Koonya (Port Arthur)
COLVILLE COTTAGE	Battery Point (Hobart)
COVE COTTAGE PENTHOUSE	Hobart
CROMWELL COTTAGE	Battery Point (Hobart)
EGMONT	Westbury
EMMA'S COTTAGE	Hamilton
FERNHILL HOST FARM	Frankford
FORGET-ME-NOT COTTAGE	Oatlands
FRANKLIN MANOR	Strahan
GATEFORTH COTTAGE	Black River (Stanley)
GEORGE'S COTTAGE	Hamilton
HARBOUR MASTER'S COTTAGE	Stanley
HAWTHORN COTTAGE ROSS	Ross
HAWTHORN VILLA	Carrick
HILLVIEW HOUSE	Launceston
HOLKHAM HOUSE	Orford
HOLLY TREE FARM	Middleton
HOLM LODGE	Bellerive (Hobart)
HUDSON COTTAGE	Ross
ISLINGTON ELEGANT PRIVATE HOTEL	Hobart
IVY COTTAGE	Launceston
KERSBROOK HOST FARM	Pioneer
KILMARNOCK HOUSE	Launceston

LAUGHTON HOUSE	Stanley
LAUREL COTTAGE	Richmond
LESTER COTTAGES	Swansea
MEREDITH HOUSE	Swansea
MOLECOMBE COTTAGE	Launceston
MONATERIC	Wiltshire (Stanley)
OATLANDS LODGE	Oatlands
OCEAN VIEW GUEST HOUSE	Ulverstone
ORANA	Lindisfarne (Hobart)
ORPLID VEGETARIAN HOST FARM	Kayena
OVER-THE-BACK	Hamilton
OYSTER BAY GUEST HOUSE	Swansea
PLOVERS RIDGE HOST FARM	Lilydale
PROSPECT HOUSE	Richmond
RIVER VIEW LODGE	Devonport
ROSE COTTAGE	Lisdillon (Swansea)
SEASCAPE	Port Arthur
SOLOMON COTTAGE	Evandale
STONEMASON'S COTTAGE	Lisdillon (Swansea)
STRATHMORE COLONIAL ACCOMMODATION	Nile
TAMAR HOUSE	Rosevears
TANTALLON LODGE	Battery Point (Hobart)
TARANNA HOUSE	Taranna (Port Arthur)
THE COTTAGE	Brighton
THE DISPENSARY	Richmond
THE OLD BAKERY INN	Launceston
THE OLD SCHOOLHOUSE	Hamilton
THE PEAR WALK COTTAGES	Lalla
TOUCHWOOD COTTAGE	Stanley
TYNWALD	New Norfolk
VICTORIA'S COTTAGE	Hamilton
WAGNER'S COTTAGES	Swansea
WARWICK COTTAGES	Hobart
WAVERLEY COTTAGE	Oatlands
WAVERLEY CROFT	Oatlands
WILMOT ARMS INN	Kempton

TASMANIAN TRAVEL CENTRES

	Telephone
MELBOURNE—256 Collins Street	(03) 653 7999
SYDNEY—129 King Street	(02) 233 2500
BRISBANE—217 Queen Street	(07) 221 2744
ADELAIDE—32 King William Street	(08) 211 7411
PERTH—100 William Street	(09) 321 2633
CANBERRA—5 Canberra Savings Centre, City Walk	(062) 47 0070
HOBART—80 Elizabeth Street	(002) 30 0211
LAUNCESTON—Cnr. Paterson & St. John Streets	(003) 32 2101
(after hours)	(003) 32 2488
DEVONPORT—18 Rooke Street	(004) 24 1526
BURNIE—48 Cattley Street	(004) 31 8111
QUEENSTOWN—39-41 Orr Street	(004) 71 1099
AUCKLAND—15th Floor, Quay Tower, Cnr. Customs and Albert Streets, Auckland, New Zealand.	79 5535
TOKYO—Sankaido Building, 8F, 9-13 Akasaka 1-chome, Minato-ku, Tokyo 107, Japan.	(03) 582 2789
LOS ANGELES—2121 Avenue of the Stars, Suite 1200T, Los Angeles, California, U.S.A. Zip Code 90067.	(213) 552 3010